All Things
ALICE

All Things ALICE

The Wit, Wisdom and Wonderland of Lewis Carroll

Linda Sunshine

Foreword by Mark Burstein, Vice President,
The Lewis Carroll Society of North America

Design by Timothy Shaner

CLARKSON POTTER/PUBLISHERS
NEW YORK

Put cats in the coffee, and mice in the tea—
And welcome Queen Alice with thirty-times-three!

—Through the Looking-Glass and What Alice Found There, 1872

Copyright © 2004 by Linda Sunshine

All rights reserved. No part of this book may be reproduced or
transmitted in any form or by any means, electronic or mechanical,
including photocopying, recording, or by information storage and
retrieval system, without permission in writing from the publisher.

Every attempt has been made to locate the copyright holders
of the material used in this book. Please let us know if any
error has been made, and we will make any necessary
changes in subsequent printings.

Credits and copyright notices appear on pages 348–351.

Published by Clarkson Potter/Publishers, New York, New York.
Member of the Crown Publishing Group,
a division of Random House, Inc.
www.crownpublishing.com

CLARKSON N. POTTER is a trademark and
POTTER and colophon are registered trademarks
of Random House, Inc.

Printed in Singapore

Library of Congress Cataloging-in-Publication Data
is available upon request.

ISBN 1-4000-5441-9

10 9 8 7 6 5 4 3 2 1

First Edition

CONTENTS

CONTENTS

CONTENTS

"Begin at the beginning," the King said gravely, "and go on till you come to the end: then stop."

—*Alice's Adventures in Wonderland*, 1865

Introduction
Uncommon Nonsense

I have spent the better part of this past year exploring the Wonderland of Lewis Carroll. Hand in hand, I joined Alice on her adventures down the rabbit hole and through the looking-glass. Re-reading these seminal works of children's literature sparked my interest in the Reverend Charles Lutwidge Dodgson and his alter ego, the totally irreverent Lewis Carroll.

It has been said that the *Alice* books have been quoted almost as often as the Bible and Shakespeare. The scholar Martin Gardner points out that the most often-quoted Carroll line is a remark made by the Red Queen: "It takes all the running you *can* do, to keep in the same place." Personally, though, I prefer when she says: "Make a remark: it's ridiculous to leave all the conversation to the pudding!" Never mind, the point is that almost any sentence from those two books, chosen at random, could stand alone as a quote, and such quotes could fill an entire book. But I soon discovered that Dodgson wrote many other works that begged to be included here.

My editorial criteria for choosing excerpts were simple: I selected what appealed to me. I leave the scholarship to the scholars. What I wanted to illustrate were the poems I loved the most, the quotes that made me laugh out loud, the scholarship that fascinated me and the historical facts about Charles L. Dodgson's life and his transformation to Lewis Carroll that revealed some insight into his genius.

Dodgson, I discovered, wrote poetry throughout his life. When he was only twelve, he began writing magazines for his family and friends. He called them *The Rectory Umbrella* and *Mischmash* and in his articles and poems are the seeds of ideas that would flourish and grow into the characters and events of Wonderland. (Think Shel Silverstein or Dr. Seuss in a waistcoat and straw hat.)

Dodgson also loved to write letters. On January 1, 1861 (when he was twenty-nine years old), he started numbering all of the letters he wrote or received. A few weeks before he died, at age 66, he numbered the last letter: 98,721. He kept a letter-writing journal that cross-referenced every letter with a brief description of its contents and wrote a pamphlet detailing his rules of letter-writing.

The letters to his child-friends are filled with Carroll's unique sense of humor and imagination, written with the sensibility of an adult who could marvel at the strangeness of language and the weirdness of grown-up behavior. Since they still have the power to delight, excerpts from the best of these letters are included in this book.

I have selected a few longer pieces by Dodgson and about him. In her 1899 memoir, Isa Bowman included a story he wrote just for her about a visit she made to Oxford. It is a marvelous example of how Carroll related to children and why they loved him in return.

Included here also are the words of other writers. There are literally thousands of books that have been written about Carroll, his works and his place in literature. Carroll fans include an incredibly diverse group of writers: Virginia Woolf, Joyce Carol Oates, John Lennon, Grace Slick and Robertson Davies, among many others.

I have selected excerpts from Carrollian scholars to introduce the works of Martin Gardner, Warren Weaver, Selwyn Goodacre, Stephanie Lovett Stoffel and others. While researching this book, I chanced upon Mark Burstein, who edits the magazine of the Lewis Carroll Society of North America. He shared with me his collection of some 3,000 books by, about or related to Lewis Carroll and contributed a fascinating foreword explaining why *Alice* has so influenced his family.

A word must be added about the art of *Alice*. We are all familiar with the work of Sir John Tenniel, who illustrated the original editions of both *Wonderland* and *Through the Looking-Glass*. Tenniel's illustrations have become classics, icons of the Victorian age and instantly recognizable to millions of readers.

In 1907, *Wonderland* fell out of copyright and publishers all over the world scrambled to produce their own editions of this bestselling book. Consequently, thousands of editions of *Alice* have been published in the past 100 years, and new versions continue to appear annually. *Alice* has captured the imagination of some of the best illustrators of this century: Arthur Rackham, Jessie Willcox Smith, Charles Folkard, Gwenydd Hudson, Marbel Lucie Atwell, Besse Pease Guttman, Salvador Dali and Ralph Steadman, to name only a few. In pulling this book together, I was somewhat limited to using only the illustrators whose work is no longer in copyright and so, unfortunately, many of the current illustrators are not included here. Yet, even with such limitations, there was still an embarrassment of riches from which to select.

I did not know much about Lewis Carroll when I started this project, but in the process of editing this book I have become a hopeless Carroll fan. Much to the annoyance of my closest friends, I have taken to working quotes from *Alice* into almost every conversation, a curiouser and curiouser habit that has generated a lot of eye rolling and long sighs from my listeners. I also recite bits of his nonsense poetry whenever I possibly can. My current dinnertime favorite is: "He thought he saw a Banker's Clerk / Descending from the bus: / He looked again, and found it was / A Hippopotamus: / 'If this should stay to dine,' he said, / 'There won't be much for us!'" You see what I mean?

I can't help it; I feel the need to share these words with everyone. In this book, I hope to pass along the joy, the wonderment and the giggles of Lewis Carroll's world. As you delve into this book, please leave your sense of logic and your grown-up attitude at the door. They are not needed here. As the Red Queen says, "When I was your age, why sometimes I believed as many as six impossible things before breakfast." So turn the page: next stop, *Wonderland*.

LINDA SUNSHINE
WINTER, 2004

Foreword
Why Lewis Carroll?

My father and I have been seriously collecting Carroll for about thirty years, a fairly benign disorder as such things go. Our assemblage, ranking high but not at the absolute pinnacle of this rarefied world, currently consists of some three thousand volumes by, about or somehow related to him. This includes the *Alice* books in sixty distinct languages and illustrations by more than seven hundred different artists, and some twelve hundred other objects—from the sublime (Alice's own accordion) to the ridiculous (Tokyo Disneyland tchotchkes)—which are so abundantly and continually being produced in various cultures.

The question is often asked of us, "Why Lewis Carroll?"

Well, first of all the *Alice* books are so wonderfully funny. And like all great humor, that means they are more expressive of the true and deeper ways of the world than that to which the "serious" can possibly aspire. These books are twin looking-glasses facing each other, like those mirrors in old-time barbershops, in whose pages infinite levels, hidden and secret treasure troves of wisdom, are unveiled upon each new reading. At the very least, some hitherto undiscovered phrase will leap from the page, rich in symbolism or suggestion.

Paradoxical, magical, elusive, inspired, the *Alice* books were the first manifestation into this world of things previously hidden in bright corners of the nursery: how absurd the world looks to children (and all naïve souls), how topsy-turvy the patterned, the "logical," turns out to be. Playfulness, madness and silliness are all essential to maintaining one's sanity in today's upside-down world.

And there's more: Mr. Dodgson himself was possessed of a fascinating and far-ranging mind. A polymath, he contributed significantly to the then-young art of photography, parlor magic, game theory, mathematics, symbolic logic and recreational games and puzzles.

In the world of collecting, Carroll provides a perfect milieu. There is an astonishing variety of artifacts available, at a wide range of cost. You can begin with just a single book, perhaps the very copy (or at least the same edition) you remember from your childhood, and the quest has begun. On the high end, there are books that sell for a million dollars and up, but the sweet news is that at whatever level you can afford, there's always something.

Many Carroll societies and groups exist around the world, by and large composed of quite intelligent people with marvelous senses of humor. Laughter always abounds at meetings, even as there is a complementary, and most welcome, academic presence. It's not like one collects seventeenth-century medical treatises: When someone finds out what exactly it is we collect there's almost always an expression of joy.

Sandor, Martin and Mark Burstein standing in front of a small fraction of their Alice *collection.*

We are also often asked, "How did this obsession begin?" In 1930, my father, Sandor, fell in love with both his first-grade teacher, who was portraying the White Rabbit in a local theater production, and the *Alice* books. Forty-four years later, he was on a trip in Portugal and his hand fell upon a colorful volume, "the only book in the store I could recognize," *Alice no País das Maravilhas*.

The collection grew, and eventually a story about it appeared in the *San Francisco Examiner*. The next day brought a telephone call: "Hello, Sandor," said the voice, "this is the White Rabbit." His first-grade teacher, some fifty years after they'd last met, had seen the story and dropped by soon thereafter!

The collecting of artifacts has been described as the last refuge of the lover, but it is also a great pleasure in and of itself. It's almost like a marriage: It takes work, sacrifice, compromise and the support and understanding of one's family, yet it can be the source of a deep and abiding exhilaration and communion. Carroll collectors often span generations, and my dearest hope is that someday my son, Martin, now two, catches this happy affliction.

MARK BURSTEIN, VICE PRESIDENT,
THE LEWIS CARROLL SOCIETY OF NORTH AMERICA

Alice's Simple Rules

A red-hot poker will burn
you if you hold it too long.

♣

If you cut your finger very deeply
with a knife, it usually bleeds.

♦

If you drink much from a bottle
marked "poison," it is almost certain
to disagree with you, sooner or later.

—*Alice's Adventures in Wonderland,* 1865

Rule 42.

All persons more than a mile high to leave the court.

"Rule 42 is the oldest rule in the book," said the King.

"Then it ought to be Number One," said Alice.

—*Alice's Adventures in Wonderland*, 1865

The Ways of Wonderland

Learn not to make personal
remarks: it's very rude.

♥

Take care of the sense and the sounds
will take care of themselves.

♦

Fight till six, and then have dinner.

♣

Keep your temper.

♠

Don't grunt; that's not at all a proper
way of expressing yourself.

—*Alice's Adventures in Wonderland*, 1865

It takes all the running you can do, to keep in the same place.

—The Red Queen, *Through the Looking-Glass and What Alice Found There*, 1872

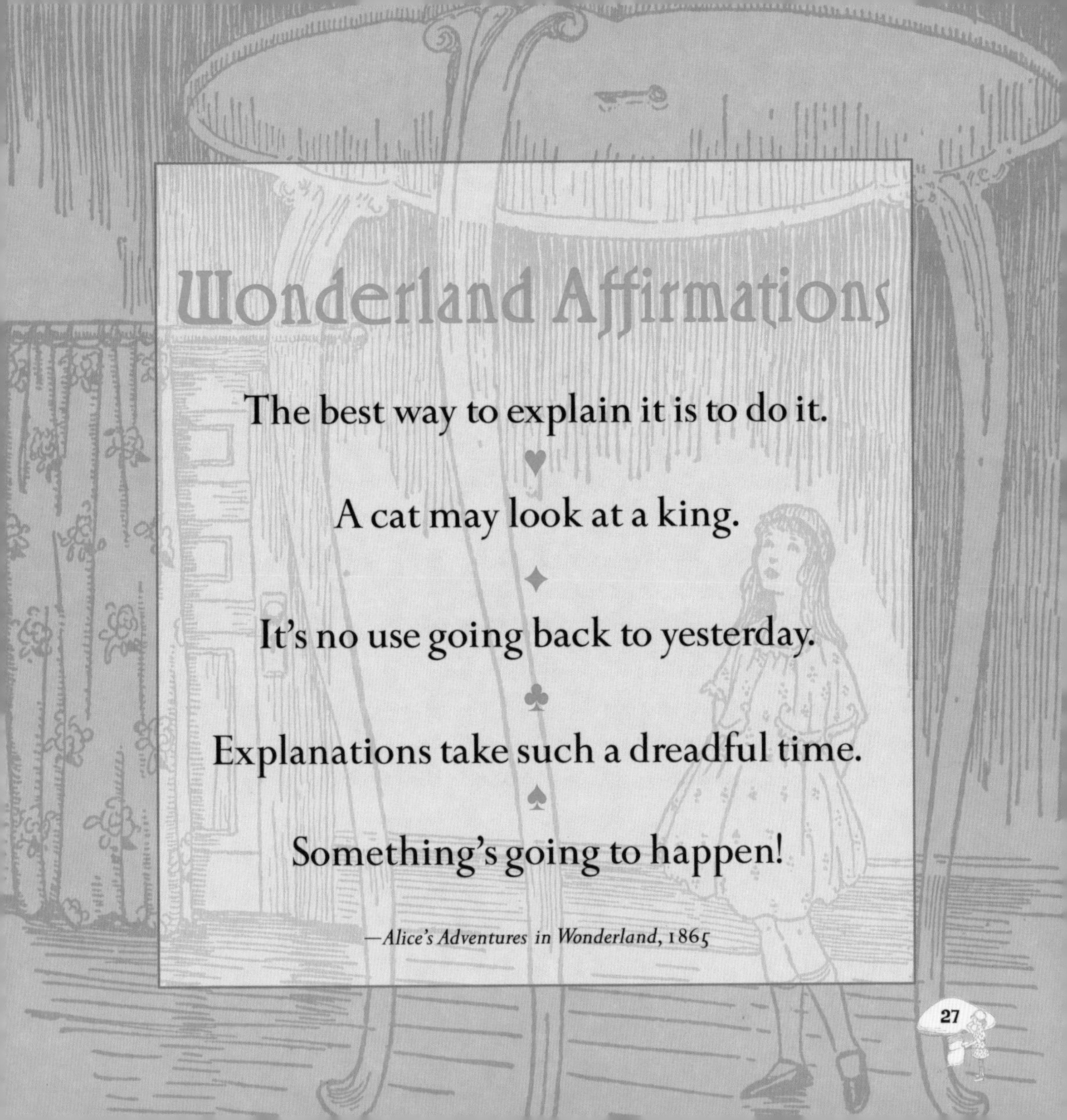

Wonderland Affirmations

The best way to explain it is to do it.

♥

A cat may look at a king.

♦

It's no use going back to yesterday.

♣

Explanations take such a dreadful time.

♠

Something's going to happen!

—*Alice's Adventures in Wonderland,* 1865

27

FRANKLIN LUCHES

Advice from the Red Queen

1 Look up, speak nicely and don't twiddle your fingers all the time. 2 Curtsey while you're thinking what to say, it saves time. 3 Open your mouth a *little* wider when you speak, and always say "Your Majesty." 4 Speak in French when you can't think of the English for a thing. 5 Turn out your toes as you walk. 6 Remember who you are! 7 Always speak the truth—think before you speak—and write it down afterwards. 8 When you've once said a thing, that fixes it, and you must take the consequences. 9 Make a remark: it's ridiculous to leave all the conversation to the pudding!

—*Through the Looking-Glass and What Alice Found There*, 1872

Second thoughts are sure of that, that nearly second thoughts.

best. (I have got to be so
all my thoughts now *are*
I have **no first thoughts,**
as a general **rule.**)

—Letter from Lewis Carroll to
Alexandra ("Xie") Kitchin,
February 15, 1880

"If it had grown up," she said to herself, "it would have made a dreadfully ugly child: but it makes rather a handsome pig, I think." And she began thinking over other children she knew, who might do very well as pigs…

—*Alice's Adventures in Wonderland*, 1865

RULES & REGULATIONS

Learn well your grammar,
And never stammer,
Write well and neatly,
And sing most sweetly,
Be enterprising,
Love early rising,
Go for walks of six miles,
Have ready quick smiles,
With lightsome laughter,
Soft, flowing after.
Drink tea, not coffee;
Never eat toffy.
Eat bread with butter.
Once more, don't stutter.
Don't waste your money,
Abstain from honey.
Shut doors behind you,
(Don't slam them, mind you),

Drink beer, not porter.
Don't enter the water
Till to swim you are able.
Sit close to the table.
Take care of a candle.
Shut a door by the handle,
Don't push with your shoulder
Until you are older.
Lose not a button.
Refuse cold mutton.
Starve your canaries.
Believe in fairies.
If you are able,
Don't have a stable
With any mangers.
Be rude to strangers.

Moral: Behave

—Charles L. Dodgson, *Useful and Instructive Poetry*, 1845

"Your Majesty must excuse her," the Red Queen said to Alice, taking one of the White Queen's hands in her own, and gently stroking it: "she means well, but she can't help saying foolish things as a general rule."

—*Through the Looking-Glass and What Alice Found There*, 1872

37

W hen I used to read fairy-tales,
thought Alice, I fancied that kind
of thing never happened, and
now here I am in the middle
of one! There ought to be a
book written about me!

—*Alice's Adventures in Wonderland*, 1865

Background: Antique postcard, circa 1900, announcing:
"The E. St. Alban's Company performance of Lewis Carroll's
Immortal Fairy Play, 'Alice in Wonderland' Featuring:
'Gorgeous Scenery, Dresses, and Sparkling Music
from The Vaudeville Theatre, London.'"

Sixteen Things TRUE About Alice

1 She was always ready to talk about her pet.
2 She found it very confusing to be so many different sizes in a day. 3 She was definitely not a serpent.
4 She did not like to eat raw eggs. 5 She did not want to go among mad people. 6 She could not remember much about ravens and writing-desks. 7 She did not live much under the sea. 8 Her favorite phrase was "Let's pretend." 9 She didn't like to confess, even to herself, that she couldn't make something out. 10 She would most like to be a Queen. 11 She was rather afraid of insects, at least the large kinds.
12 She liked birthday presents best.
13 She didn't like belonging to another person's dream. 14 She was always rather fond of scolding herself. 15 She was always ready for a little argument. 16 She got very used to queer things happening.

—*Alice's Adventures in Wonderland*, 1865

Morpheus Says...

You take the blue pill and the story ends. You wake in your bed and you believe whatever you want to believe. You take the red pill and you stay in Wonderland and I show you how deep the rabbit-hole goes.

—Andy & Larry Wachowski,
The Matrix, 1999

Thoughts on the Way Down

"After such a fall as this, I shall think nothing of tumbling downstairs! How brave they'll all think me at home!"

♣

"I wonder what Latitude or Longitude I've got to?"

♦

"I wonder if I shall fall right *through* the earth! How funny it'll seem to come out among the people that walk with their heads downwards!"

♠

"Do cats eat bats? Do bats eat cats?"

—*Alice's Adventures in Wonderland*, 1865

45

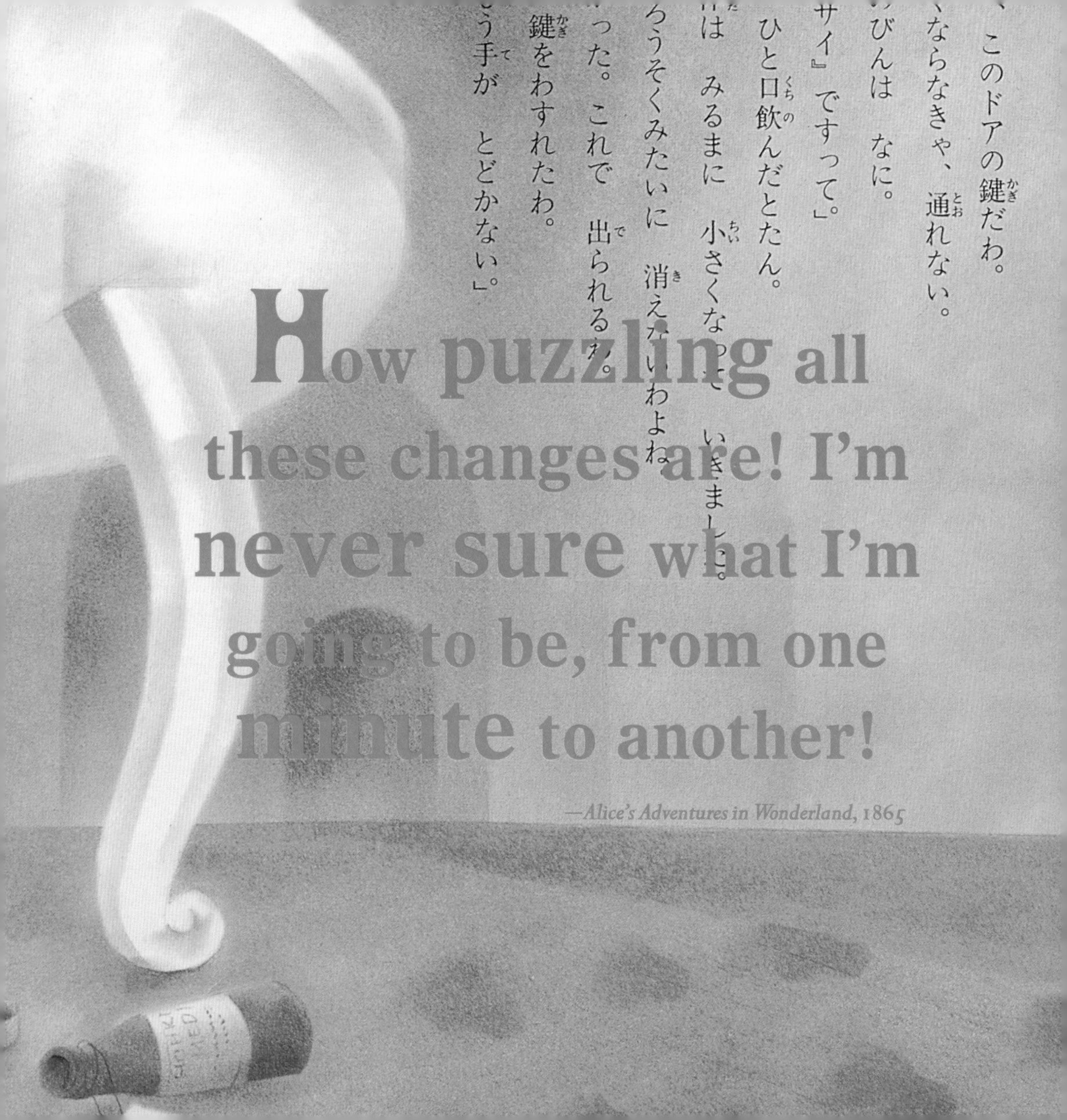

、このドアの鍵だわ。

、ならなきゃ、通れない。

、びんは なに。

サイ』ですって。』

ひと口飲んだとたん。

は みるまに 小さくなって いきました。

うそくみたいに 消えないわよね

った。これで 出られるわ。

鍵をわすれたわ。

う手が とどかない」

How puzzling all these changes are! I'm never sure what I'm going to be, from one minute to another!

—Alice's Adventures in Wonderland, 1865

THE FIRST QUESTION

"How am I to get in?"
asked Alice again,
in a louder tone.

"*Are* you to get in
at all?" said the
Footman. "That's
the first question,
you know."

—*Alice's Adventures in Wonderland*, 1865

Beware of logic. It is an organized way of going wrong with confidence.

—Dr. C. F. Kettering, noted inventor and for many years head of the General Motors Research Laboratory

"**B**ut I don't want to go among mad people," Alice remarked.

"Oh, you can't help that," said the Cat: "we're all mad here. I'm mad. You're mad."

"How do you know I'm mad?" said Alice.

"You must be," said the Cat, "or you wouldn't have come here."

—*Alice's Adventures in Wonderland*, 1865

52

"**C**ome, there's no use in crying like that!" said Alice to herself rather sharply. "I advise you to leave off this minute!" She generally gave herself very good advice (though she very seldom followed it), and sometimes she scolded herself so severely as to bring tears into her eyes; and once she remembered trying to box her own ears for having cheated herself in a game of croquet she was playing against herself, for this curious child was very fond of pretending to be two people. "But it's no use now," thought poor Alice, "to pretend to be two people! Why, there's hardly enough of me left to make one respectable person!"

—*Alice's Adventures in Wonderland*, 1865

Consider what a
 great girl you are.
Consider what a long way
 you've come today.
Consider what o'clock it is.
Consider anything,
 only don't cry!

—The White Queen, *Through the Looking-Glass
and What Alice Found There*, 1872

MY OWN

"I wish I hadn't cried so as she swam about, out. "I shall be punished being drowned in my

—*Alice's Adventures in Wonderland, 1865*

much!" said Alice, trying to find her way for it now, I suppose, by own tears!"

Suppose *you* were **swimming** about, in a Pool of your own Tears: and **suppose** somebody began talking to you about lesson-books and bottles of medicine, wouldn't you **swim away** as hard as you could go?

—*The Nursery Alice*, 1890

"**W**ould you tell me, please, which way I ought to go from here?"

"That depends a good deal on where you want to get to," said the Cat.

ALICE IN WONDERLAND -

SEE STORY ON OTHER SIDE

"I don't much care where—" said Alice.

"Then it doesn't matter which way you go," said the Cat.

"—so long as I get *somewhere*," Alice added as an explanation.

"Oh, you're sure to do that," said the Cat, "if you only walk long enough."

—Alice's Adventures in Wonderland, 1865

The Road Goes Ever On

Lewis Carroll and the Cheshire Cat did not mean to reassure Alice that her amusing wanderings would result in her achieving something greater, but they do. Alice says that she doesn't much care which way she walks. Therein lies the truth of her journey. The road goes ever on, in Tolkien's immortal words, and we all have faith deep in our bones that it will take us where we need to go, if only we keep walking long enough.

—Stephanie Lovett Stoffel,
The Art of Alice in Wonderland, 1998

Y<small>OU</small> couldn't deny that, even
if you tried with both hands.

—The Red Queen, *Through the Looking-Glass
and What Alice Found There*, 1872

"Dear, dear! How queer everything is today! And yesterday things went on just as usual. I wonder if I've changed in the night? Let me think: *was* I the same when I got up this morning? I almost think I can remember feeling a little different. But if I'm not the same, the next question is 'Who in the world am I?' Ah, *that's* the great puzzle!"

—*Alice's Adventures in Wonderland*, 1865

IN EVERY CORNER

She grew, and she grew and she grew. And in a very short time the room was full of Alice: just in the same way as a jar is full of jam! There was Alice all the way up to the ceiling: and Alice in every corner of the room!

—*The Nursery Alice,* 1890

White Rabbit

One pill makes you larger
And one pill makes you small
And the ones that mother gives you
Don't do anything at all
Go ask Alice
When she's ten feet tall

And if you go chasing rabbits
And you know you're going to fall
Tell 'em a hookah-smoking caterpillar
Has given you the call
Call Alice
When she was just small

When men on the chessboard
Get up and tell you where to go
And you just had some kind of mushroom
And your mind is moving slow
Go ask Alice,
I think she'll know

When logic and proportion
Have fallen softly dead
And the white knight is talking backwards
And the red queen's "off with her head!"

Remember what the Dormouse said
"Feed your head! Feed your head!
Feed your head!"

—Grace Slick, Jefferson Airplane, *Surrealistic Pillow*, 1967

72

Go Ask Alice

The great advantage of dinner-parties is that it helps you to see your friends. If you want to see a man, offer him something to eat. The same rule with a mouse.

—*Sylvie and Bruno Concluded*, 1893

A DORMOUSE IN A TEAPOT

The last time Alice saw them, they were trying to put the Dormouse into the teapot.

—Alice's Adventures in Wonderland, 1865

I am indebted to Roger Green for the surprising information that Victorian children actually had dormice as pets, keeping them in old teapots filled with grass or hay.

—Footnote from Martin Gardner,
The Annotated Alice, 2000

Say What You Mean

"**Y**ou should say what you mean," the March Hare went on.

"I do," Alice hastily replied; "at least— at least I mean what I say—that's the same thing, you know."

"Not the same thing a bit!" said the Hatter. "You might just as well say that 'I see what I eat' is the same thing as 'I eat what I see'!"

"You might just as well say," added the March Hare, "that 'I like what I get' is the same thing as 'I get what I like'!"

"You might just as well say," added the Dormouse, who seemed to be talking in his sleep, "that 'I breathe when I sleep' is the same thing as 'I sleep when I breathe'!"

—*Alice's Adventures in Wonderland*, 1865

Mad as a Hatter

The phrases "mad as a hatter" and "mad as a March Hare" were common at the time Carroll wrote, and of course that was why he created the two characters. "Mad as a hatter" may have been a corruption of the earlier "mad as an adder" but more likely owes its origin to the fact that until recently hatters actually did go mad. The mercury used in curing felt (there are now laws against its use in most states and in parts of Europe) was a common cause of mercury poisoning. Victims developed a tremor called "hatter's shakes," which affected their eyes and limbs and addled their speech. In advanced stages they developed hallucinations and other psychotic symptoms.

—Martin Gardner, *The Annotated Alice*, 2000

Lost in Translation

Warren Weaver (1894–1978) was an eminent *Alice* collector and the author of *Alice in Many Tongues*. During his long career, Weaver was a foundation executive for the Rockefeller Foundation, a position that involved a great deal of traveling. Collecting foreign editions of the *Alice* books sparked his interest in the problems of translation. As an experiment, he took the famous passage from the Mad Tea Party and sent it to native speakers from other countries who really understood English. He asked his specialists to translate the foreign editions back into English without consulting the original book. The results were nothing short of astonishing and proved, beyond a doubt, that a great deal can be lost in translation.

THE ORIGINAL

"Take some more tea," the March Hare said to Alice, very earnestly.

"I've had nothing yet," Alice replied in an offended tone, "so I can't take more."

"You mean you can't take less," said the Hatter: "it's very easy to take more than nothing."

PIDGIN

"Drink a little more tea, eh?" March Hare spoke directly to Alice.

"I didn't have any tea in the first place," said Alice crossly, "so how can I have more?"

"You must take better care of your tea," said the Hatter. "If there is not tea, you can get more; but just because half of it is gone, you can't waste the other half."

SPANISH

"Have a little more tea," said the March Hare to Alice, with extreme solicitude.

"I have not taken any yet," Alice answered in the tone of an offended person; "I do not know how I am going to have more."

"Do you want to say that you cannot take less?" said the Hatter. "But it is easy to take less than nothing."

SWAHILI

"Drink some more tea, my child," Tortoise said to Alice.

Alice replied, "I haven't yet drunk my tea, not a drop, so I can't drink any more."

And Alice put some tea into a cup and drank, and asked again why those three children lived at the bottom of a well.

—Translations from *Alice in Many Tongues*, Warren Weaver, 1964

LEWIS CARROLL
ALICJA W KRAINIE CZARÓW
Ilustrowała Olga Siemaszko

"**I** beg your pardon?" said Alice.

"It isn't respectable to beg," said the King.

—*Alice's Adventures in Wonderland*, 1865

December 10, 1877

<u>At last</u> I've succeeded in forgetting you!
It's been a hard job, but I took 6 "lessons-
in-forgetting," at a half-a-crown a lesson.
After three lessons, I forgot my own name,
and I forgot to go for the next lesson.
So the Professor said I was getting on very
well: "but I hope," he added, "you won't
forget to pay for the lessons!" I said <u>that</u>
would depend on whether the other lessons
were good or not: and do you know? the
last of the 6 lessons was so good that
I forgot <u>everything</u>! I forgot who I was:
I forgot to eat my dinner: and, so far,
I've quite forgotten to pay the man. I
will give you his address, as perhaps you
would like to take lessons from him, so
as to forget <u>me</u>.

ENGLAND

Less and Less Lessons

I. "Why did you call him Tortoise, if he wasn't one?" Alice asked.

"We called him Tortoise because he taught us," said the Mock Turtle.

II. The Mock Turtle said: "No wise fish would go anywhere without a porpoise."

III. "And how many hours a day did you do lessons?" said Alice, in a hurry to change the subject.

"Ten hours the first day," said the Mock Turtle: "nine the next and so on."

"What a curious plan!" exclaimed Alice.

"That's the reason they're called lessons," the Gryphon remarked: "because they lessen from day to day."

—*Alice's Adventures in Wonderland,* 1865

Look at the Picture

They very soon came upon a Gryphon, lying fast asleep in the sun. (If you don't know what a Gryphon is, look at the picture.)

—Alice's Adventures in Wonderland, 1865

Uglification

"I never heard of Uglification," Alice ventured to say. "What is it?"

The Gryphon lifted up both its paws in surprise. "What! Never heard of uglifying!" it exclaimed. "You know what to beautify is, I suppose?"

"Yes," said Alice doubtfully: "it means—to—make—anything—prettier."

"Well, then," the Gryphon went on, "if you don't know what to uglify is, you *are* a simpleton."

—Alice's Adventures in Wonderland, 1865

"Everybody says 'come on!' here," thought Alice. "I never was so ordered about before, in all my life, never!"

—*Alice's Adventures in Wonderland*, 1865

For, you see, so many out-of-the-way things had happened lately, that Alice had begun to think that very few things were really impossible.

—*Alice's Adventures in Wonderland*, 1865

ALICE'S PLAN

Grow to my right size again. Find my way into that lovely garden.

—*Alice's Adventures in Wonderland*, 1865

95

Alice didn't like being criticized, so she began asking questions. "Aren't you sometimes frightened at being planted out here, with nobody to take care of you?"

"There's the tree in the middle," said the Rose: "what else is it good for?"

"But what could it do, if any danger came?" Alice asked.

"It says 'Bough-wough!' cried a Daisy: "that's why its branches are called boughs!"

—*Through the Looking-Glass and What Alice Found There,* 1872

Love at First Sight

My discovery of poetry—or of verse—came when I was very young. In 1946, for my eighth birthday, my grandmother gave me a beautiful illustrated copy of Lewis Carroll's *Alice in Wonderland* and *Through the Looking-Glass*. This book . . . was the great treasure of my childhood. This was love at first sight. (I may have fallen in love with the very concept of Book, too.) Like Alice, I plummeted down the rabbit hole and/or climbed boldly through the mirror into the looking-glass world and, in a manner of speaking, never entirely returned to real life. My heroine was this strangely assured, courageous young girl of about my age. I would not have guessed she was of another culture and distinctly of another economic class; I most admired her for her curiosity (which mirrored my own) and for the equanimity with which she confronted dream and nightmare situations (as I could never have done). Within a few months I'd memorized much of both *Alice* books, and could recite, for anyone willing to listen, nearly all the poems.

—Joyce Carol Oates, *American Poetry Review*
(Vol. 28, Issue 6), Nov./Dec. 1999

"And what is the use of a book," thought Alice, "without pictures or conversations?"
—*Alice's Adventures in Wonderland*, 1865

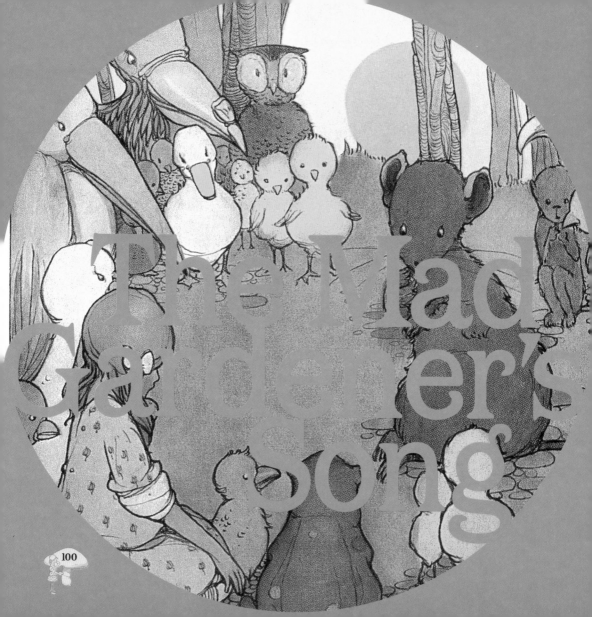

The Mad
Gardener's
Song

He thought he saw an Elephant,
That practiced on a fife:
He looked again, and found it was
A letter from his wife.
"At length I realise," he said,
"The bitterness of Life!"

He thought he saw a Buffalo
Upon the chimney-piece:
He looked again, and found it was
His Sister's Husband's Niece.
"Unless you leave this house," he said,
"I'll send for the Police."

He thought he saw a Rattlesnake
That questioned him in Greek:
He looked again, and found it was
The Middle of Next Week.
"The one thing I regret," he said,
"Is that it cannot speak!"

He thought he saw a Banker's Clerk
Descending from the bus:
He looked again, and found it was
A Hippopotamus:
"If this should stay to dine," he said,
"There won't be much for us!"

He thought he saw a Kangaroo
That worked a coffee-mill:
He looked again and found it was
A Vegetable-Pill.
"Were I to swallow this," he said,
"I should be very ill!"

He thought he saw a Coach-and-Four
That stood beside his bed:
He looked again, and found it was
A Bear without a Head.
"Poor thing," he said, "poor silly thing!
It's waiting to be fed!"

He thought he saw an Albatross
That fluttered round the lamp:
He looked again, and found it was
A Penny-Postage-Stamp.
"You'd best be getting home," he said:
"The nights are very damp!"

He thought he saw a Garden-Door
That opened with a key:
He looked again, and found it was
A Double Rule of Three:
"And all its mystery," he said,
"Is clear as day to me!"

He thought he saw an Argument
That proved he was the Pope:
He looked again, and found it was
A Bar of Mottled Soap.
"A fact so dread," he faintly said,
"Extinguishes all hope!"

—*Sylvie and Bruno*, 1889

from Charles L. Dodgson
to Mary MacDonald

May 23, 1864

It has been so frightfully hot here that I've been almost too weak to hold a pen, and even if I had been able, there was no ink—it had all evaporated into a cloud of black steam, and in that state it has been floating about the room, inking the walls and ceiling till they're hardly fit to be seen: to-day it is cooler, and a little has come back into the ink-bottle in the form of black snow.

from Charles L. Dodgson
to Bert Coote

June 9 (?1877)

I've got no ink. You don't believe it? Ah, you should have seen the ink there was in my days! Why, you had only to pour a little of it on the paper, and it went on by itself! This ink is so stupid, if you begin a word for it, it can't even finish it by itself.

April 10, 1871

No, no! I cannot write a line,
    I cannot write a word:
The thoughts I think appear in ink
    So shockingly absurd!

To wander in an empty cave
    Is fruitless work, 'tis said:
What must it be for one like me
    To wander in his head?

You say that I'm "to write a verse" —
    O Maggie, put it quite
The other way, and kindly say
    That I'm "averse to write."

from Charles L. Dodgson
to Wilton Rix

May 20, 1885

Ever since this painful fact has been forced
upon me, I have not slept more than 8
hours a night, and have not been able to
eat more than 3 meals a day.

107

"You don't know much," said the Duchess; "and that's a fact."

—*Alice's Adventures in Wonderland*, 1865

"**The Duchess!** The Duchess! Oh my dear paws! Oh my fur and **whiskers!** She'll get me executed, as sure as ferrets are **ferrets!**"

—The White Rabbit, *Alice's Adventures in Wonderland*, 1865

"I've a **right** to think," said Alice sharply, for she was beginning to feel a little worried. "Just about as much right," said the Duchess, "as pigs have **to fly**."

—Alice's Adventures in Wonderland, 1865

Speak roughly to your little boy,
And beat him when he sneezes:
He only does it to annoy,
Because he knows it teases.

CHORUS (in which the cook and the baby joined):
"Wow! wow! wow!"

I speak severely to my boy,
I beat him when he sneezes;
For he can thoroughly enjoy
The pepper when he pleases!

CHORUS
"Wow! wow! wow!"

—Alice's Adventures in Wonderland, 1865

114

The Duchess's Morals

1 Everything's got a moral, if only you can find it. 2 Flamingoes and mustard both bite. And the moral of that is—"Birds of a feather flock together." 3 The more there is of mine, the less there is of yours. 4 Oh, 'tis love, 'tis love that makes the world go round! 5 "Be what you would seem to be"—or if you'd like it put more simply— "Never imagine yourself not to be otherwise than what it might appear to others that what you were or might have been was not otherwise than what you had been would have appeared to them to be otherwise." 6 If everybody minded their own business, the world would go round a deal faster than it does.

—*Alice's Adventures in Wonderland*, 1865

"You're thinking about something, my dear, and that makes you forget to talk. I can't tell you just now what the moral of that is, but I shall remember it in a bit."

—The Duchess, *Alice's Adventures in Wonderland*, 1865

The Ugly Duchess

I t has been speculated that illustrator John Tenniel, and many subsequent illustrators of the *Alice* books, modeled the Duchess in the story after Margaret, Countess of Carinthia and Tyrol.

Born in 1318, she had the reputation of being the ugliest woman in history and was nicknamed "Maultasche," which means "pocket-mouth." Legend has it that she was a woman of great power and evil.

When Margaret's father, Henry, Count of Tyrol and Duke of Carinthia, died in 1335, Holy Roman Emperor Louis IV gave Carinthia to the Hapsburgs and tried to take Tyrol from Margaret and her husband, John Henry. Her subjects remained loyal and Margaret's father-in-law forced the emperor to restore the throne to his son. But the nobles of the court found John Henry's rule to be oppressive and Margaret herself thought her husband both stupid and incompetent. She expelled him from her country and had their marriage annulled by Louis IV.

In 1342, Margaret married Louis's son, the Margrave of Brandenburg. The annulment and subsequent marriage offended her subjects but Mar-

garet stood by her new husband. After his death in 1361 and the death of their son, Meinhard, she abdicated in 1363, leaving her throne to the Hapsburgs. She died in 1369.

Lion Feuchtwanger's novel, *The Ugly Duchess* (1928), chronicles her sad life. Her portrait by Quentin Matsys (*right*) currently hangs in the National Gallery in London.

"I make you a present of everything I've said as yet."
"A cheap sort of present!" thought Alice. "I'm glad they don't give birthday presents like that!"

—*Alice's Adventures in Wonderland*, 1865

January 22, 1878

I may as well tell you of the things I like, so whenever you want to give me a birthday present (my birthday comes once every seven years, on the fifth Tuesday in April) you will know what to give me. Well, I like very much indeed, a little mustard with a bit of beef spread thinly under it; and I like brown sugar — only it should have some apple pudding mixed up with it to keep it from being too sweet; but perhaps what I like best of all is salt, with some soup poured over it. The use of the soup is to hinder the salt from being too dry; and it helps to melt it.

"What *is* an un-birthday present?"
"A present given when it isn't your birthday, of course."

—Humpty Dumpty, *Through the Looking-Glass and What Alice Found There*, 1872

"The horror of that moment," the King went on, "I shall never, never forget!"

"You will, though," the Queen said, "if you don't make a memorandum of it."

—*Through the Looking-Glass and What Alice Found There*, 1872

Q's Queen of Hearts and the
tarts that she made.
(She will ruin her beautiful
frock, I'm afraid!)
The Jack of Hearts took them
against the Queen's wishes,
But you can't really blame him,
they smelled so delicious.

—Tony Sarg, *Tony Sarg's Alphabet*, n.d.

QUEEN OF HEARTS

The Queen of Hearts,
She made some Tarts,
All on a Summer's Day:

The Knave of Hearts,
He stole those Tarts,
And took them
right away.

131

The King of Hearts,
Called for those Tarts,
And beat the Knave
full score.

The Knave of Hearts,
Brought back those Tarts
And vowed he'd steal
no more.

According to the *Oxford English Dictionary*, the Queen of Hearts verse first appeared in 1782 and was almost identical to the first seven lines quoted on page 131, which Carroll used in *Alice's Adventures in Wonderland*. The additional lines here are from an 1881 book illustrated by Randolph Caldecott.

Three Sides of an Argument

SIDE ONE: The executioner's argument was that you couldn't cut off a head unless there was a body to cut it off from: that he had never had to do such a thing before, and he wasn't going to begin at *his* time of life.

♥

SIDE TWO: The King's argument was that anything that had a head could be beheaded.

♥

SIDE THREE: The Queen's argument was that if something wasn't done about it in less than no time she'd have everybody executed, all round.

—*Alice's Adventures in Wonderland*, 1865

134

The Queen

How close parts of Carroll's fantasy came to Victorian reality is suggested in Stanley Weintraub's biography of Queen Victoria, which takes as an epigraph the Queen of Heart's statement, "I don't know what you mean by your way. All the ways round here belong to *me*" as personifying Queen Victoria's autocratic and fanciful behavior. Some scenes from Victoria's life read as though they come from the *Alice* books. Ceremonial dinners, for example, were cleared away while guests were still eating, the instant the Queen, who was served first and ate fast, had finished her portion, leaving visiting aristocrats hungry and humiliated. When arguments were not going her way, Victoria flirted with madness, clutching her head and crying, "My reason! My reason!" The Queen was haughtily remote from her subjects, never read a newspaper, opposed reform, and rigorously supported social hierarchies. She was so pompous that her son, Edward VII, joked that she was reluctant to go to heaven because "there the angels would precede her."

—Jackie Wullschläger, *Inventing Wonderland*, 1995

136

No, no! Sentence first—verdict afterwards!

—The Queen of Hearts

May 23, 1891

In <u>some</u> ways, you know, people that <u>don't</u> exist, are much nicer than people that <u>do</u>. For instance, people that <u>don't</u> exist are never <u>cross</u>: and they never <u>contradict</u> you: and they <u>never tread on your toes</u>! Oh, they're <u>ever</u> so much nicer than people that <u>do</u> exist! However, never mind: you can't help existing, you know: and I daresay you're <u>just</u> as nice as if you didn't.

"I haven't opened it yet," said the White Rabbit; "but it seems to be a letter, written by the prisoner to—to somebody."

"It must have been that," said the King, "unless it was written to nobody, which isn't usual, you know."

—*Alice's Adventures in Wonderland*, 1865

138

"Queens never make bargains."

—*Through the Looking-Glass and What Alice Found There*, 1872

"There's no use trying," Alice said, "one *can't* believe impossible things."

"I daresay you haven't had much practice," said the Queen. "When I was your age, I always did it for half-an-hour a day. Why, sometimes I've believed as many as six impossible things before breakfast."

— Through the Looking-Glass and What Alice Found There, 1872

from Charles L. Dodgson
to Mary MacDonald

May 23, 1864

If you set to work to believe everything, you will tire out the believing-muscles of your mind, and then you'll be so weak you won't be able to believe the simplest true things. Only last week a friend of mine set to work to believe Jack-the-giant-killer. He managed to do it, but he was so exhausted by it that when I told him it was raining (which was true) he <u>couldn't</u> believe it, but rushed out into the street without his hat or umbrella, the consequence of which was his hair got seriously damp, and one curl didn't recover its right shape for nearly 2 days.

Believe in Me

"Do you know, I always thought Unicorns were fabulous monsters, too? I never saw one alive before!"

"Well, now that we *have* seen each other," said the Unicorn, "if you'll believe in me, I'll believe in you. Is that a bargain?"

—*Through the Looking-Glass and What Alice Found There*, 1872

All Round You

"What is it you want to buy?" the Sheep said at last, looking up for a moment from her knitting.

"I don't *quite* know yet," Alice said very gently. "I should like to look all round me first, if I might."

"You may look in front of you, and on both sides, if you like," said the Sheep; "but you can't look *all* round you—unless you've got eyes at the back of your head."

—*Through the Looking-Glass and What Alice Found There*, 1872

Lucy in the Sky

PLAYBOY: Where did *Lucy in the Sky* come from?

JOHN LENNON: My son Julian came in one day
with a picture he painted about a school
friend of his named Lucy. He had sketched
in some stars in the sky and called it *Lucy in
the Sky with Diamonds*. Simple.

♥

PLAYBOY: The other images in the song weren't
drug-inspired?

JOHN LENNON: The images were from *Alice in
Wonderland*. It was Alice in the boat. She is
buying an egg and it turns into a sheep and
the next minute they are rowing in a rowing
boat somewhere and I was visualizing that.

—*Playboy* Magazine, January 1981

H for

HUMPTY DUMPTY

H is Humpty, who sat on a wall.
And when he fell off—oh, my!
    what a fall.
I hate to inform you what
    really befell,
For of poor Humpty was left
    but a shell.

—Tony Sarg, *Tony Sarg's Alphabet*, n.d.

"**M**y *name* is Alice, but—"

"It's a stupid name enough!" Humpty Dumpty interrupted impatiently. "What does it mean?"

"*Must* a name mean something?" Alice asked doubtfully.

"Of course it must," Humpty Dumpty said with a short laugh: "*my* name means the shape I am—and a good handsome shape it is, too. With a name like yours, you might be any shape, almost."

—*Through the Looking-Glass and What Alice Found There*, 1872

Words have a temper, some of them—particularly verbs: they're the proudest—adjectives you can do anything with, but not verbs— however, *I* can manage the whole lot of them! Impenetrability! That's what *I* say!

—Humpty Dumpty, *Through the Looking-Glass and What Alice Found There*, 1872

152

SOME EGGS ARE VERY PRETTY

"I said you looked like an egg, Sir,"
Alice gently explained. "And some
eggs are very pretty, you know," she
added, hoping to turn her remark
into a sort of compliment.

—*Through the Looking-Glass and What Alice Found There*, 1872

There are things
would give

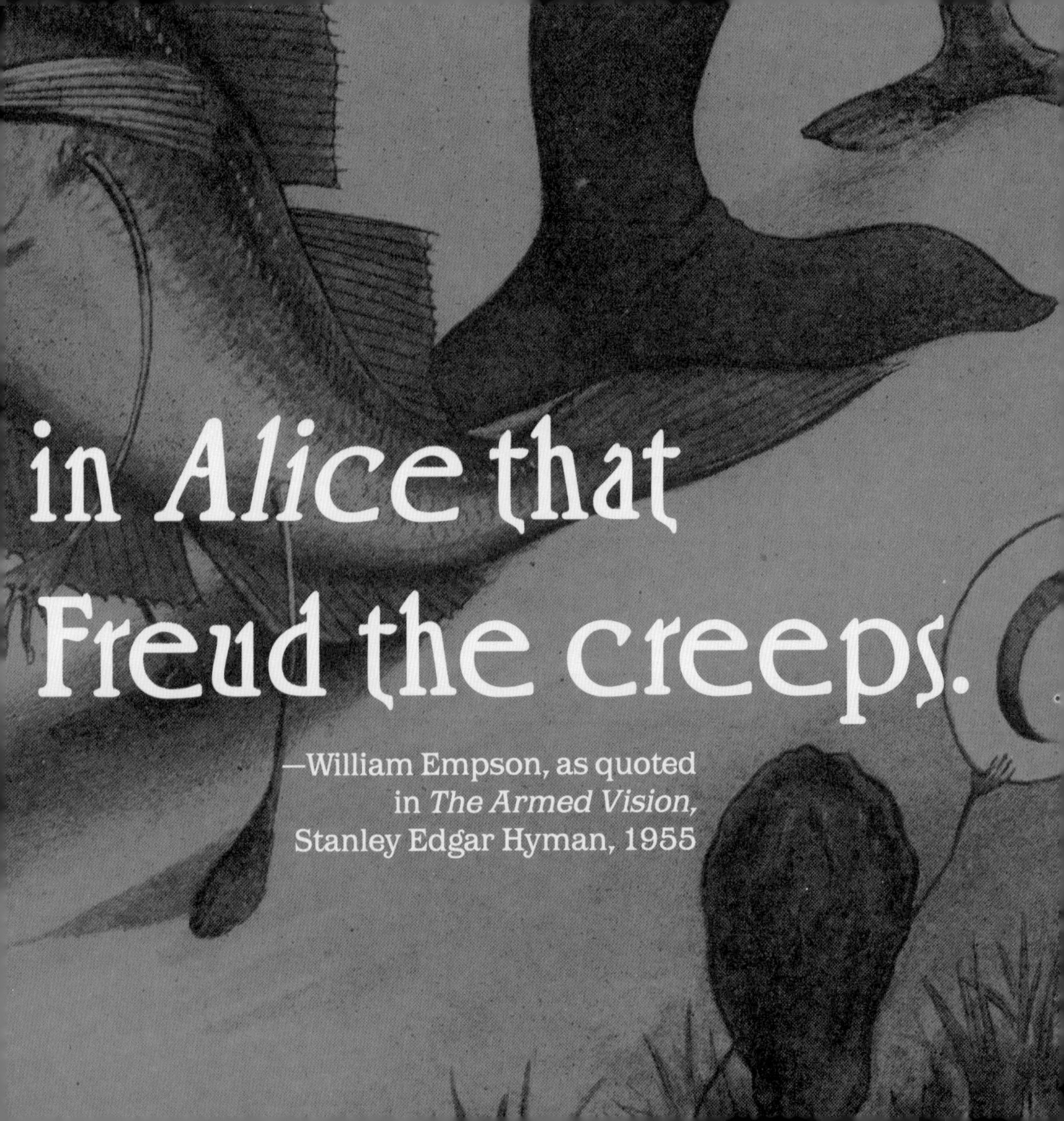

in *Alice* that
Freud the creeps.

—William Empson, as quoted
in *The Armed Vision*,
Stanley Edgar Hyman, 1955

Explain Yourself!

The Caterpillar and Alice looked at each other for some time in silence.

"Who are you?" said the Caterpillar.

This was not an encouraging opening for a conversation. Alice replied, rather shyly, "I—I hardly know, sir, just at present—at least I know who I was when I got up this morning, but I think I must have been changed several times since then."

"What do you mean by that?" said the Caterpillar sternly. "Explain yourself!"

"I can't explain myself I'm afraid, sir," said Alice, "because I'm not myself, you see."

—*Alice's Adventures in Wonderland*, 1865

Father William

"You are old, Father William,"
    the young man said,
"And your hair has become very white;
And yet you incessantly
    stand on your head—
Do you think, at your age, it is right?"

"In my youth,"
    Father William replied to his son,
"I feared it might injure the brain;
But, now that I'm perfectly sure
    I have none,
Why, I do it again and again."

"You are old," said the youth,
    "as I mentioned before,
And have grown most uncommonly fat;
Yet you turned a back-somersault
    in at the door—
Pray, what is the reason of that?"

"In my youth," said the sage,
    as he shook his grey locks,
  "I kept all my limbs very supple
By the use of this ointment —
    one shilling the box —
  Allow me to sell you a couple?"

"You are old," said the youth,
    "and your jaws are too weak
  For anything tougher than suet;
Yet you finished the goose,
    with the bones and the beak —
  Pray, how did you manage to do it?"

"In my youth," said his father,
    "I took to the law,
And argued each case with my wife;
And the muscular strength,
    which it gave to my jaw
Has lasted the rest of my life."

"You are old," said the youth,
    "one would hardly suppose
  That your eye was as steady as ever;
Yet you balanced an eel
    on the end of your nose —
  What made you so awfully clever?"

"I have answered three questions,
    and that is enough",
  Said his father. "Don't give yourself airs!
Do you think I can listen all day
    to such stuff?
  Be off, or I'll kick you down-stairs!"

—*Alice's Adventures in Wonderland*, 1865

"**I**t is **wrong** from beginning to end," said the Caterpillar, decidedly; and there was **silence** for some minutes.

—*Alice's Adventures in Wonderland*, 1865

Our Cat Dinah

"I wish I could show you our cat Dinah. I think you'd take a fancy to cats, if you could only see her. She is such a dear quiet thing," Alice went on, half to herself, as she swam lazily about in the pool, "and she sits purring so nicely by the fire, licking her paws and washing her face—and she is such a nice soft thing to nurse—and she's such a capital one for catching mice—oh, I beg your pardon!" cried Alice again, for this time the Mouse was bristling all over, and she felt certain it must be really offended. "We won't talk about her any more if you'd rather not."

—*Alice's Adventures in Wonderland*, 1865

The Kitten

The kitten had been having a grand game of romps with the ball of worsted Alice had been trying to wind up, and had been rolling it up and down till it had all come undone again; and there it was, spread over the hearth-rug, all knots and tangles, with the kitten running after its own tail in the middle.

—*Through the Looking-Glass and What Alice Found There*, 1872

ALICE & DINAH

"**I** wish you wouldn't keep appearing and vanishing so suddenly: you make one quite giddy!"

"All right," said the Cat; and this time it vanished quite slowly, beginning with the end of the tail, and ending with the grin, which remained some time after the rest of it had gone.

"Well! I've often seen a cat without a grin," thought Alice; "but a grin without a cat! It's the most curious thing I ever saw in all my life!"

—*Alice's Adventures in Wonderland*, 1865

Rat-tail Jelly and Buttered Mice

A very curious thing happened to me at half-past four, yesterday. Three visitors came knocking at my door, begging me to let them in. And when I opened the door, who do you think they were? You'll never guess. Why, they were three cats! Wasn't it curious? However, they all looked so cross and disagreeable that I took up the first thing I could lay my hands on (which happened to be the rolling-pin) and knocked them all down as flat as pancakes! "If you come knocking at my door," I said, "I shall come knocking on *your* heads." That was fair, wasn't it?

Of course I did not leave them lying flat on the ground like dried flowers: no, I picked them up, and I was as kind as I could be to them. I lent them the portfolio for a bed—they wouldn't have been comfortable in a real bed, you know: they were too thin—but they were quite happy between sheets of blotting paper—and each of them had a pen-wiper for a pillow. Well, then I went to bed: but first I lent them the three dinner-bells, to ring if they wanted anything in the night.

You know I have *three* dinner-bells—the first (which is the largest) is rung when dinner is *nearly* ready; the second (which is rather larger) is rung when it is quite ready; and the third (which is as large as the other two put together) is rung all the time I am at dinner. Well, I told them they might ring if they happened to want anything—and, as they rang *all* the bells *all* night, I suppose they did want something or other, only I was too sleepy to attend to them.

In the morning I gave them some rat-tail jelly and buttered mice for breakfast, and they were as discontented as they could be. They wanted some boiled pelican, but of course I knew it wouldn't be good for them. So

all I said was, "Go to Number Two, Finborough Road, and ask for Agnes Hughes, and if it's really good for you, she'll give you some." Then I shook hands with them all, and wished them all good-bye, and drove them up the chimney. They seemed very sorry to go, and they took the bells and the portfolio with them. I didn't find this out till after they had gone, and then I was sorry too.

Ah! The dear creatures! Ever since that night they first came, they have never left me.

And they are so kind and thoughtful! Do you know, when I had gone for a walk the other day, they got all my books out of the bookcase, and opened them on the floor, to be ready for me to read. They opened them all at page 50, because they thought that would be a nice useful page to begin at. It was rather unfortunate, though: because they took my bottle of glue, and tried to glue pictures upon the ceiling (which they thought would please me), and by accident they spilt a quantity of it all over the books. So when they were shut up and put by, the leaves all stuck together, and I can never read page 50 again in any of them!

However, they meant it very kindly, so I wasn't angry. I gave them each a spoonful of ink as a treat; but they were ungrateful for that, and made dreadful faces. But, of course, as it was given them as a treat, they had to drink it. One of them has turned black since: it was a white cat to begin with.

—ADAPTED FROM LETTERS WRITTEN TO AGNES HUGHES
AND HER SISTER, AMY HUGHES (1871)

John Lennon

PLAYBOY: Were you able to find others to share your visions with?

JOHN LENNON: Only dead people in books. Lewis Carroll, certain paintings.

◆

PLAYBOY: What about the walrus itself?

JOHN LENNON: It's from "The Walrus and the Carpenter" in *Alice in Wonderland*. To me, it was a beautiful poem. It never dawned on me that Lewis Carroll was commenting on the capitalist and social system. I never went into that bit about what he really meant, like people are doing with the Beatles' work. Later, I went back and looked at it and realized that the walrus was the bad guy and the carpenter was the good guy. I thought, Oh, s**t, I picked the wrong guy. I should have said, "I am the carpenter." But that wouldn't have been the same, would it?

—*Playboy* Magazine,
January 1981

Ray Ellis and His Orchestra

COLUMBIA
GUARANTEED HIGH-FIDELITY

LP

ELLIS IN WONDERLAND

YOU ARE NEVER FAR AWAY FROM ME
HOW ABOUT YOU
FOR ALL WE KNOW   P.S. I LOVE YOU
WHEN I FALL IN LOVE   LOVE IS A SIMPLE THING
36-26-36   YOU'RE MY GIRL
ALONE TOGETHER   POOR BUTTERFLY
MILK AND HONEY   TRUST IN ME

The sun was shining on the sea,
  Shining with all his might:
He did his very best to make
  The billows smooth and bright—
And this was odd, because it was
  The middle of the night.

The moon was shining sulkily,
  Because she thought the sun
Had got no business to be there
  After the day was done—
"It's very rude of him," she said,
  "To come and spoil the fun!"

The sea was wet as wet could be,
  The sands were dry as dry.
You could not see a cloud, because
  No cloud was in the sky:
No birds were flying overhead—
  There were no birds to fly.

The Walrus and the Carpenter
  Were walking close at hand:
They wept like anything to see
  Such quantities of sand:
"If this were only cleared away,"
  They said, "it would be grand!"

"If seven maids with seven mops
  Swept it for half a year,
Do you suppose," the Walrus said,
  "That they could get it clear?"
"I doubt it," said the Carpenter,
  And shed a bitter tear.

"O Oysters, come and walk with us!"
  The Walrus did beseech.
"A pleasant walk, a pleasant talk,
  Along the briny beach:
We cannot do with more than four
  To give a hand to each."

The eldest Oyster looked at him,
  But never a word he said:
The eldest Oyster winked his eye,
  And shook his heavy head—
Meaning to say he did not choose
  To leave the oyster-bed.

But four young Oysters hurried up,
  All eager for the treat:
Their coats were brushed, their
    faces washed,
  Their shoes were clean and neat—
And this was odd, because, you know,
  They hadn't any feet.

Four other Oysters followed them,
  And yet another four;
And thick and fast they came at last,
  And more, and more, and more—
All hopping through the frothy waves,
  And scrambling to the shore.

The Walrus and the Carpenter
  Walked on a mile or so,
And then they rested on a rock
  Conveniently low:
And all the little Oysters stood
  And waited in a row.

"The time has come," the Walrus said,
  "To talk of many things:
Of shoes—and ships—and sealing wax—
  Of cabbages—and kings—
And why the sea is boiling hot—
  And whether pigs have wings."

"But wait a bit," the Oysters cried,
  "Before we have our chat;
For some of us are out of breath,
  And all of us are fat!"
"No hurry!" said the Carpenter.
  They thanked him much for that.

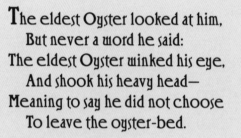

"A loaf of bread," the Walrus said,
    "Is what we chiefly need:
Pepper and vinegar besides
    Are very good indeed—
Now, if you're ready, Oysters dear,
    We can begin to feed."

"But not on us!" the Oysters cried,
    Turning a little blue.
"After such kindness, that would be
    A dismal thing to do!"
"The night is fine," the Walrus said.
    "Do you admire the view?

"It was so kind of you to come!
    And you are very nice!"
The Carpenter said nothing but
    "Cut us another slice.
I wish you were not quite so deaf—
    I've had to ask you twice!"

"It seems a shame," the Walrus said,
    "To play them such a trick.
After we've brought them out so far,
    And made them trot so quick!"
The Carpenter said nothing but
    "The butter's spread too thick!"

"I weep for you," the Walrus said:
    "I deeply sympathize."
With sobs and tears he sorted out
    Those of the largest size,
Holding his pocket-handkerchief
    Before his streaming eyes.

"O Oysters," said the Carpenter,
    "You've had a pleasant run!
Shall we be trotting home again?"
    But answer came there none—
And this was scarcely odd, because
    They'd eaten every one.

—*Through the Looking-Glass and What Alice Found There*, 1872

179

Alice had been to the seaside once in her life, and had come to the general conclusion, that wherever you go to on the English coast you find a number of bathing machines in the sea, some children digging in the sand with wooden spades, then a row of lodging houses, and behind them a railway station.

—*Alice's Adventures in Wonderland, 1865*

Only Lewis Carroll has down as a child sees it, children laugh.

shown us the world upside
and has made us laugh as

—VIRGINIA WOOLF

Time Line to Wonderland

1832 Charles Lutwidge Dodgson is born in Daresbury, Cheshire. He is the third child in a family that would eventually grow to include eleven children.

1851 Dodgson is an undergraduate at Christ Church, Oxford.

1852 Alice Liddell is born in London.

1855 Alice's father, Henry George Liddell, is appointed Dean of Christ Church and moves his family into the Deanery where Dodgson can see them playing in the garden. In print, Dodgson uses his pseudonym, Lewis Carroll, for the first time.

1856 On April 25, Alice makes her first appearance in the diaries of Charles Dodgson. On that day, he went to the Deanery with a friend to photograph the cathedral. "The 3 little girls were in the garden most of the time," Dodgson notes, "and we became excellent friends: we tried to group them in the foreground of the picture but they were not patient sitters."

C. L. Dodgson, 1857

1861 Dodgson is ordained Deacon in the Church of England.

1862 On July 4, Dodgson, Robinson Duckworth and the three Liddell sisters, Alice, Lorina and Edith, take a boat ride on their way to a summer picnic. To amuse the children, Dodgson invents a story about a girl named Alice.

1864 Dodgson, at the urging of little Alice, writes and illustrates his story "without the least idea," he would later say, "that it would ever be published." On November 26, Dodgson gives Alice Liddell a vellum-bound book called *Alice's Adventures under Ground*, which includes 37 of his own illustrations. The book is inscribed: "A Christmas Gift to a Dear Child, in Memory of a Summer Day." Dodgson's friend George MacDonald urges him to publish the book.

1865 Dodgson revises the story, deleting private jokes and family references, adding two chapters and doubling the word count from about 18,000 to 35,000 words. He hires John Tenniel to illustrate the book for a fee of £138, changes the title to *Alice's Adventures in Wonderland* and uses his "pen name" Lewis Carroll to protect his reputation in producing more serious books. The book is published by Macmillan and Co. in London, on July 4, 1865, three years after that golden afternoon with the Liddell children. It is withdrawn from publication because Tenniel is displeased with the poor quality of printing, and a new edition is published in November 1865 (but dated 1866). The unbound copies of the rejected first printing are sent to America and appear under the Appleton imprint.

> For, with all her knowledge of history, Alice had no very clear notion how long ago anything had happened.
>
> —*Alice's Adventures in Wonderland*, 1865

Time Line to Wonderland

1868 Carroll hires Tenniel to illustrate his second book about Alice.

1871 Carroll publishes Alice's further adventures in *Through the Looking-Glass and What Alice Found There* (the book is dated 1872).

1870s and **1880s** The two *Alice* books continue to be enormously successful both in England and around the world. Several mathematical works appear under the name C. L. Dodgson; Carroll publishes *The Hunting of the Snark, Sylvie and Bruno* and many other essays and satirical pieces.

1880 Alice Liddell marries Reginald Hargreaves.

1885 Carroll requests and receives permission from the now-married Alice Liddell Hargreaves to allow Macmillan to publish a facsimile of the 1864 manuscript of *Alice's Adventures under Ground*. He writes that *Alice's Adventures in Wonderland* has sold more than 120,000 copies, including foreign editions.

1886 A facsimile edition of 5,000 copies of *Alice's Adventures under Ground* is published in December.

1898 Charles Dodgson dies on January 14 and is buried in Guildford. By then, *Alice's Adventures in Wonderland* has sold roughly 180,000 copies, earning Carroll about £18,000 (the equivalent of $100,000 today) for that book alone, at a time when there was virtually no income tax.

Time Line to Wonderland

1907 The copyright on *Alice's Adventures in Wonderland* expires, generating a flood of new editions and illustrations that continues to today.

1928 Alice Hargreaves sells, at auction, her copy of *Alice's Adventures under Ground* for £15,000, the highest price ever paid for a literary manuscript at the time. It is purchased by an American and transported across the ocean.

1934 Alice Hargreaves dies in Hampshire.

1946 The Hargreaves book is purchased by a group of Americans and given to Britain in gratitude for their participation during World War II. The priceless handwritten book is currently on display in London at the British Library.

1998 In December, one of Carroll's personal copies of *Alice's Adventures in Wonderland* (one of 23 original 1865 editions known to exist) fetches $1.54 million at auction. At the same auction, Carroll's own sepia-toned photograph of the original Alice, age 6, sells for $62,000.

2004 Today visitors still flock to Oxford in search of Alice and Lewis Carroll. Carroll societies abound and the books continue to sell throughout the world.

187

January 27, 1878

But really you mustn't go on sending me such a shower of presents. I shall be wet through with them soon: and then I shall catch cold, and the doctor will say, "You ought to have held up your umbrella when you knew your birthday was coming."

Drawings by the young C. L. Dodgson before he was Lewis Carroll. LEFT: *An illustration from* The Rectory Umbrella, *c. 1849, a magazine he wrote for his family and friends when he was in his teens.* ABOVE: *Dodgson's caricature of his sisters at play.*

189

MY FANCY

I painted her a gushing thing,
With years perhaps a score;
I little thought to find they were
At least a dozen more;
My fancy gave her eyes of blue
A curly auburn head:
I came to find the blue a green,
The auburn turned to red.

She boxed my ears this morning,
They tingled very much;
I own that I could wish her
A somewhat lighter touch;
And if you were to ask me how
Her charms might be improved,
I would not have them added to,
But just a few removed!

She has the bear's ethereal grace,
The bland hyena's laugh,
The footstep of an elephant,
The neck of a giraffe;
I love her still, believe me.
Though my heart its passion hides;
"She's all my fancy painted her,"
But oh! how much besides!

—Charles L. Dodgson, *College Rhymes*, 1862

About Lewis Carroll

In *The Annotated Alice,* Martin Gardner describes Charles L. Dodgson as a "fussy, prim, fastidious, cranky, kind and gentle bachelor whose life was sexless, uneventful and happy." He was a thin man who walked with a jerky gait. His passions included magic tricks, photography, playing all kinds of games and inventing riddles, games and puzzles. He became a lecturer of mathematics at Oxford, despite a lifelong stutter that made him shy in front of people.

The *Alice* books brought international fame, though Carroll hated publicity and refused to publish any photographs of himself. "Nothing would be more unpleasant to me than to have my face known to strangers," he once lamented. Letters addressed to Lewis Carroll were marked "not known" and promptly returned. After the first publication of *Wonderland* and *Through the Looking-Glass,* Carroll went on to write almost 300 other works of poetry, prose, scholarship, mathematics, satire, religion, invention and much more.

He died at Guildford, Surrey, on January 14, 1898, at exactly 2:30 P.M., of influenza, two weeks before his sixty-sixth birthday. Many of his papers were destroyed—some burned—almost immediately after his death. Volumes of his diaries were misplaced. Most of his belongings were auctioned off.

Today, Lewis Carroll and his writings are revered around the globe.

192

Lewis Carroll was a man of medium height. When I knew him his hair was a silver-grey, rather longer than it was the fashion to wear, and his eyes were a deep blue. He was clean shaven, and, as he walked, always seemed a little unsteady in his gait. At Oxford, he was a well-known figure. He was a little eccentric in his clothes. In the coldest weather he would never wear an overcoat, and he had a curious habit of always wearing, in all seasons of the year, a pair of grey and black cotton gloves.

—Isa Bowman, *The Story of Lewis Carroll*, 1900

Tea and Travel

He was very particular about his tea, which he always made himself, and in order that it should draw properly he would walk about the room swinging the teapot from side to side for exactly ten minutes. The idea of the grave professor promenading his book-lined study and carefully waving a teapot to and fro may seem ridiculous, but all the minutiae of life received an extreme attention in his hands, and after the first surprise one came quickly to realize the convenience that his carefulness ensured.

Before starting on a railway journey, for instance (and how delightful were railway journeys in the company of Lewis Carroll), he used to map out every minute of the time that we were to take on the way. The details of the journey completed, he would exactly calculate the amount of money that must be spent, and, in different partitions of the two purses that he carried, arrange the various sums that would be necessary for cabs, porters, newspapers, refreshments and other expenses of a journey. It was wonderful how much trouble he saved himself *en route* by this making ready beforehand. Lewis Carroll was never driven half-frantic on a station platform because he had to change a sovereign to buy a penny paper while the train was on the verge of starting. With him journeys were always comfortable.

—Isa Bowman, *The Story of Lewis Carroll*, 1900

Bits and Scraps

We used to sit on the big sofa on each side of him while he told us stories, illustrating them by pencil or ink drawings as he went along ... He seemed to have an endless store of these fantastical stories, which he made up as he told them, drawing busily on a large sheet of paper all the time.

—Alice Liddell, *Cornhill Magazine*, July 1932

One thing that made his stories particularly charming to a child, was that he often took his cue from her remarks—a question would set him off on quite a new trail of ideas, so that one felt one had somehow helped to make the story, and it seemed a personal possession. It was the most lovely nonsense conceivable, and I naturally reveled in it. His vivid imagination would fly from one subject to another, and was never tied down in any way by the probabilities of life.

—Gertrude Chataway, a child friend to whom Carroll dedicated *The Hunting of the Snark*, 1876

196

lice and *Through the Looking-Glass* are made up almost wholly of bits and scraps, single ideas which came of themselves. In writing it [*Alice's Adventures in Wonderland*] out, I added many fresh ideas, which seemed to grow out of themselves upon the original stock; and many more were added when, years afterwards, I wrote it all over again for publication; but (this may interest some readers of *Alice* to know) every such idea and nearly every word of the dialogue *came of itself*. Sometimes an idea comes at night, when I have had to get up and strike a light to note it down but whenever or however it comes, *it comes of itself*. I cannot set invention going like a clock, by any voluntary winding up; nor do I believe that any original writing (and what other writing is worth preserving?) was ever so produced. . . . Periodically I have received courteous letters from strangers begging to know whether [it] is an allegory, or contains some hidden moral, or is a political satire; and for all such questions I have but one answer, "*I don't know!*"

—Lewis Carroll, April 1887

LEFT: *C. L. Dodgson photograph of the three Liddell sisters, Edith, Lorina and Alice, 1858.* RIGHT: *Photograph of Mary Hilton Badcock taken by Lewis Carroll, c. 1860. It was once thought that little Mary was the model for Tenniel's drawing of Alice.*

197

A Fit of Giggles

But just when custom and ceremony should most incline me towards worship, I may have to contend with a fit of the giggles. Was that what ailed Lewis Carroll, I wonder? Religion and mathematics, two realms in which humor seems to be wholly out of place, drove him to write the *Alice* books.

—Robertson Davies, *The Rebel Angels*, 1981

The Voyage to Godstow

The beginning of *Alice in Wonderland* was told to me one summer afternoon when the sun was so hot we landed in the meadows down the river, deserting the boat to take refuge in the only bit of shade to be found, which was under a newly made hayrick. Here from all three of us, my sisters and myself, came the old petition, "Tell us a story" and Mr. Dodgson began it.

Sometimes to tease us, Mr. Dodgson would stop and say suddenly, "That's all till next time."

"Oh," we would cry, "it's not bedtime already!" and he would go on. Another time the story would begin in the boat and Mr. Dodgson would pretend to fall asleep in the middle, to our great dismay.

—Alice Liddell Hargreaves,
The New York Times, April 4, 1928

I rowed *stroke* and he rowed *bow* in the famous Long Voyage to Godstow, when the three Miss Liddells were our passengers, and the story was actually composed and *spoken over my shoulder* for the benefit of

Alice Liddell, who was acting as "ox" of our gig. I remember turning round and saying, "Dodgson, is this an extempore romance of yours?" And he replied, "Yes, I'm inventing as we go along." I also well remember how, when we had conducted the three children back to the Deanery, Alice said, as she bade us good-night, "Oh, Mr. Dodgson, I wish you would write out Alice's adventures for me." He said he should try, and he afterwards told me that he sat up nearly the whole night, committing to a MS. book his recollections of the drolleries with which he had enlivened the afternoon. He added illustrations of his own, and presented the volume, which used to often be seen on the drawing-room table at the Deanery.

—The Reverend Duckworth, *The Lewis Carroll Picture Book*, 1899

LEFT *and* ABOVE: *Photographs by C. L. Dodgson of Alice Liddell at the age of six (in 1858) and seventeen (in 1870) in the last photo he ever took of her.* RIGHT: *Photograph of Alice Liddell Hargreaves, at eighty, in 1932 (two years before she died), during her first and only trip to America, to celebrate the centenary of Lewis Carroll's birth.*

201

A child, a very child is she,
Whose dream of Heaven is still to be
At Home: for Home is Bliss.

—Dedication, *The Nursery Alice*, 1889

D odgson invented "Lewis Carroll" in 1856, when he was twenty-four and contributing to the *Comic Times*. He offered the editor, Mr. Edmund Yates, four alternative pseudonyms. They were:

Edgar Cuthwellis or *Edgar U. C. Westhill* *(both anagrams of Charles Lutwidge)*

Louis Carroll or *Lewis Carroll (derived from Lutwidge = Ludovic = Louis, and Carroll, from the Latin name for Charles, Carolus)*

Six years later, on June 10, 1864, after he had completed his first *Alice* book, Dodgson wrote to Tom Taylor about possible titles. "Here are the other names I have thought of," he wrote:

Alice among the   (*elves*
                   (*goblins*

          (*hours*   (*elfland*
Alice's   (*doings*   in   (*wonderland*
          (*adventures*

Question: Would Alice have had the same magic if it had been known as *Alice's Hours in Elfland* by Edgar U. C. Westhill?

BACKGROUND: *Painting of the three Liddell sisters by Charles L. Dodgson, 1862, from the Lovett Collection, Winston-Salem.*

Many a day we had rowed together on that quiet stream—the three little maidens and I—and many a fairy tale had been extemporized for their benefit ... That was many a year ago, but I distinctly remember, now as I write, how, in a desperate attempt to strike out some new line of fairy-lore, I had sent my heroine straight down a rabbit-hole, to begin with, without the least idea of what was to happen afterwards. And so, to please a child I loved (I don't remember any other motive), I printed in manuscript, and illustrated with my own crude designs—designs that rebelled against every law of Anatomy or Art (for I had never had a lesson in drawing)—the book which I have just had published in facsimile ...

Stand forth, then, from the shadowy past, "Alice," the child of my dreams. Full many a year has slipped away, since that "golden afternoon" that gave thee birth, but I can call it up almost as clearly as if it were yesterday—the cloudless blue above, the watery mirror below, the boat drifting idly on its way, the tinkle of the drops that fell from our oars, as they waved so sleepily to and fro, and (the one bright gleam of life in all the slumberous scene) the three eager faces, hungry for news of fairy-land, and who would not be said "nay" to: from whose lips "Tell us a story, please," had all the stern immutability of Fate!

—Lewis Carroll, "Alice on the Stage," *The Theatre*, April 1887

LEFT: *Josephine Hutchinson as Alice, New York, 1933.*

from Charles L. Dodgson
to Mary E. Manners

December 5, 1885

Dear Madam,

Permit me to offer you my sincere thanks
for the very sweet verses you have written
about my dream-child (named after a real
Alice, but none the less a dream-child) and
her Wonderland. That children love the book
is a very precious thought to me, and next
to their love I value the sympathy of those
who come with a child's heart to what I
have tried to write about a child's thoughts.
Next to what conversing with an angel
might be — for it is hard to imagine
it, comes, I think, the privilege of having
a real child's thoughts uttered to one. I
have known some few real children (you have,
too, I am sure), and their friendship is a
blessing and a help in life.

The Looking-Glass Story

As children, we lived in Onslow Square and used to play in the garden behind the houses. Charles Dodgson used to stay with an old uncle there, and walk up and down, his hands behind him, on the strip of lawn. One day, hearing my name, he called me to him saying, "So you are another Alice. I am very fond of Alices. Would you like to come and see something which is rather puzzling?" We followed him into his house which opened, as ours did, upon the garden, into a room full of furniture with a tall mirror standing across one corner.

"Now," he said, giving me an orange, "first tell me which hand you have got that in."

"The right," I said.

"Now," he said, "go and stand before that glass, and tell me which hand the little girl you see there has got it in."

After some perplexed contemplation, I said, "The left hand."

"Exactly," he said, "and how do you explain that?"

I couldn't explain it, but seeing that some solution was expected, I ventured, "If I was on the other side of the glass, wouldn't the orange still be in my right hand?" I can remember his laugh.

"Well done, little Alice," he said. "The best answer I've had yet."

I heard no more then, but in after years was told that he said that had given him his first idea for *Through the Looking-Glass*, a copy of which, together with each of his other books, he regularly sent me.

—Alice Raikes, a distant cousin of Dodgson, *The Times* (London), January 22, 1932

presents Jane Asher as "Alice" in

Through the Looking-Glass

by
LEWIS CARROLL   Adapted by Douglas Cleverdon

The Alice Make-Over

In *Through the Looking-Glass*, the sequel to *Alice's Adventures in Wonderland*, Sir John Tenniel added a headband (*right*) to Alice's hairstyle. In the first book (*left*), Alice's hair had hung loose and flowing. Upon publication of *Through the Looking-Glass* in 1872, the headband became an instant fashion craze and every little British girl began wearing them. Even today, headbands are called "Alice bands" throughout England.

210

Those Horrid Hurdy-Gurdies!

My mother bids me
bind my hair,

And not go about
such a figure;

It's a bother, of course,
but what do I care?

I shall do as I please
when I'm bigger.

—College Rhymes, 1861

213

"I hope you've got your hair well fastened on?" he continued, as they set off.

"Only in the usual way," Alice said, smiling.

"That's hardly enough," he said, anxiously. "You see the wind is so very strong here. It's as strong as soup."

"Have you invented a plan for keeping the hair from being blown off?" Alice enquired.

"Not yet," said the Knight. "But I've got a plan for keeping it from falling off."

"I should like to hear it, very much."

"First you take an up-right stick," said the Knight. "Then you make your hair creep up it, like a fruit-tree. Now the reason hair falls off is because it hangs down—things never fall upwards, you know. It's a plan of my own invention. You may try it if you like."

—*Through the Looking-Glass and What Alice Found There,* 1872

Portraits & Inventions

I send a little thing to give you an idea of what I look like when I'm lecturing. The merest sketch, you will allow—yet still I think there's something grand in the expression of the brow and in the action of the hand.

—Letter to Margaret Cunnynghame, January 30, 1868

ABOVE: C. L. Dodgson self-portrait, 1868.

As his diaries show, he also thought well of his little inventions—and he was always inventing something: a memoria technica for the logarithms of all primes under 100; a game of arithmetical croquet; a rule for finding the day of the week for any date of the month; a substitute for glue; a system of proportional representation; a method of controlling the carriage traffic at Covent Garden; an apparatus for making notes in the dark; an improved steering gear for a tricycle; and he always sought publication for his light verse. But when it came to the one thing which he did superbly well, where he was without a rival—namely, telling stories to children—the thought of himself, of publication and immortal fame, never seems to have entered his head.

—W. H. Auden, "Today's 'Wonder-World' Needs Alice," *New York Times Magazine*, July 1, 1962

Unlike Any Other Man

Lewis Carroll was as unlike any other man as his books were unlike any other author's books… Carroll was a wit, a gentleman, a bore and an egotist—and, like Hans Andersen, a spoilt child. It is recorded of Andersen that he actually shed tears, even in late life, should the cake at tea be handed to anyone before he chose the largest slice. Carroll was not selfish, but a liberal-handed philanthropist, but his egoism was all but second childhood.

To meet him and to work for him was to me a great treat. I put up with his eccentricities—real ones, not sham like mine. I put up with a good deal of boredom, for he was a bore at times, and I worked over seven years with his illustrations, in which the actual working hours would not have occupied me more than seven weeks. I treated him as a problem, and I solved him, and had he lived I would probably have still worked with him. He remunerated me liberally for my work . . . his gratitude was overwhelming.

—Harry Furniss, *Confessions of a Caricaturist*, 1902

LEFT: *Portrait of C. L. Dodgson by Harry Furniss, who illustrated both the* Sylvie and Bruno *books.* ABOVE: *Furniss's illustrations of Alice have only been published previously in an anthology called* The Book of Knowledge, 1911.

217

McLuhan on Alice

Lewis Carroll took the nineteenth century into a dream world that was as startling as that of [Hieronymus] Bosch, but built on reverse principles. *Alice in Wonderland* offers as norm that continuous time and space that had created consternation in the Renaissance. Pervading this uniform Euclidean world of familiar space-and-time, Carroll drove a fantasia of discontinuous space-and-time that anticipated Kafka, Joyce and Eliot.

Carroll, the mathematical contemporary of Clerk Maxwell, was quite *avant-garde* enough to know about the non-Euclidean geometries coming into vogue in his time. He gave the confident Victorians a playful foretaste of Einsteinian time-and-space in *Alice in Wonderland*. Bosch had provided his era a foretaste of the new continuous time-and-space of uniform perspective. Bosch looked ahead to the modern world with horror, as Shakespeare did in *King Lear*, and as Pope did in *The Dunciad*. But Lewis Carroll greeted the electronic age of space-time with a cheer.

—Marshall McLuhan, *Understanding Media*, 1964

Obituary

Few would have imagined that the quiet, reserved mathematician, a bachelor who all his life was remarkable for his shyness and dislike of publicity, possessed the qualities necessary to produce a work which has stood the test of time of more than 30 years, and still captivates young and old alike by its quaint and original genius.

—*The Times* (London), Obituary for Lewis Carroll, 1898

Original of Carroll's Alice Lands on Soil of New World

Mrs. Hargreaves, 80 Next Week, Faces Reporters—Her Favorite Character? "The Cheshire Cat," She Says

THE REAL ALICE IN WONDERLAND

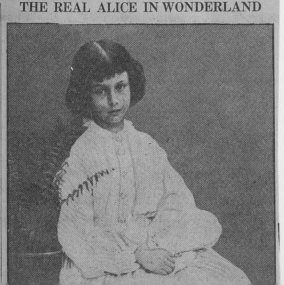

NEW YORK, April 29 (AP)—An English gentlewoman who will be 80 years old next week, had a strenuous welcome as the original Alice in Wonderland, when she arrived on the Berengaria to-day.

A quiet figure, in black broadtail coat trimmed with gray squirrel, and carrying a comfortably big tapestry handbag, Mrs. Reginald Hargreaves of Cufnels, near Southampton, England, at first sight gave little suggestion of the little girl who listened wide-eyed to the fascinating nonsense stories by the Rev. Charles Lutwidge Dodgson, deacon of Christ Church and lecturer in mathe-

Ceremonies will be held at the university on May 4, her birthday. She was unable to come to America last Jan. 26, the birthday of Carroll.

Reporters asked her what was her favorite character in Alice in Wonderland. Prof. J. Enrique Zanetti, chairman of the Lewis Carroll centenary committee at Columbia, suggested it must be Alice herself.

"No, it's the Cheshire cat," she laughed in reply.

"Why?" they wanted to know.

There wasn't any why. It was just so.

Capt. Caryl Hargreaves, her tall son, sat by her side and answered some of the questions for her.

Of course nobody ever could have guessed that the story told to Alice Liddell and her sisters, Lorina and Edith,

Remembering Alice Liddell

After Alice grew up, there was very little contact between her and Dodgson. A certain coolness became apparent between him and the Dean and Mrs. Liddell who perhaps disapproved of his possible interest in marrying Alice. She was just seventeen when he photographed her for the last time. Alice asked Dodgson to be godfather to her son, but he refused, and the only letter I have from Dodgson to Alice after she was married is a formal note asking her to tea when she was visiting the Deanery for the last time. During the middle period of Alice's life she was not much affected by the Dodgson relationship, but as she grew older and the *Alice* books gained increasing fame, she became an object of curiosity. Usually this embarrassed her: "I went to a meeting yesterday and after it was over the lady who addressed us came up and said, 'I must shake hands with the real Alice,' and after a few inane remarks she asked, 'Did you know Mr. Dodgson?' Well, I ask you . . ."

—Mary Jean St. Clair (Alice Liddell's granddaughter),
Foreword, *Alice's Adventures under Ground*, facsimile edition, 1985

LEFT: *Newspaper announcing the arrival of Alice Hargreaves in America, 1932.*
ABOVE: *Publicity photo of Alice in America, 1932.*

221

Mary Poppins in Wonderland

Carroll I am convinced, was Carroll solely because he was Dodgson. Contrariwise, Dodgson would always have been Dodgson if Carroll had never existed. But Dodgson, you say—and I see by your reddening cheek that you are a Carroll man—was a staid, dull, quiet fellow, a dry old stick of a mathematician, whereas Carroll—!

I know, I know—the same old story. Carroll must sit in the hall of fame and poor old Dodgson nowhere. I cannot agree. Mathematician he was indeed, but who other than a mathematician knows so much about dimensions? And are not adventures in dimensions the whole stuff of Carroll's writings?

As I see it, it was Dodgson who had those great adventures. Carroll merely followed him round, recording the delicious data; a Boswell, in fact, taking notes of a tour in some rarefied highland. Dodgson kept Carroll always in the background, you'll notice. One does not, after all, take one's secretary in to society, and there are good grounds for believing that Dodgson looked upon Carroll as somewhat his social inferior.

—Pamela Travers, creator of the Mary Poppins stories,
A Review of Useful and Instructive Poetry, 1954,
publication unknown

December 15, 1875

Then it was time for us to go to the train, and who do you think came to the station to see us off? You would never guess, so I must tell you. There were two very dear friends of mine, who happen to be here just now, and beg to be allowed to sign this letter as

Your affectionate friends,
Lewis Carroll and C.L. Dodgson

Alice at Auction

A first edition of the immortal "Alice's Adventures in Wonderland," dated 1865, bound in vellum, and with a manuscript poem by the author on the fly leaf, went for £50. This copy is unique, inasmuch as it is undoubtedly a private copy of the late author's, submitted to him before the publication of the recognized first edition in 1866. Another copy exactly similar, without a poem, realized £24.

—Oxford newspaper, 11 May 1898

NEW YORK (AP) — Lewis Carroll's personal copy of "Alice's Adventures in Wonderland," one of six original 1865 editions known to exist, fetched a record $1.54 million at auction . . . The anonymous buyer's final price was a record for a children's book and a nineteenth-century work of literature, said Francis Wahlgren, Christie's head of books and manuscripts. The record had been $1.2 million for a sale in London of William Blake's "Songs of Innocence and Experience."

Bound in red Moroccan leather, the book . . . has the writer's own lavender-ink notations and editing marks, and contains 10 original drawings by his famed illustrator, John Tenniel . . .

—Richard Pyle, December 10, 1998

Oh My Ears and Whiskers!

Antiquarian book dealer and LCSNA founding member Justin G. Schiller, as we have all been reading, recently put his personal collection of Carrolliana up for auction at Christie's (December 9). The headlines have been generated about Carroll's personal copy of the 1865 *Wonderland* but there were 37 other items sold as well . . . The following abbreviated list indicates the prices realized:

1. 1866 Appleton edition of *Wonderland*, $43,700
2. 1869 first French *Wonderland*, $20,700
3. Alice Hargreaves' copy of the Nabokov translation, $11,500
4. A first edition of *Looking-Glass*, inscribed by "C.L. Dodgson, alias Lewis Carroll," $36,800
5. Eight original photos of the Macdonald children, $27,600
6. Sepia-toned photograph of the original Alice, age 6, $62,000 (*photo at right*)

"The" item of media interest was the record-setting copy of *Wonderland*. This particular copy that sold for $1.54 million was purchased by Justin Schiller at an auction in Paris in 1980 for an unbelievably low price of $56,000.

—Mark Burstein, *Knight Letter #59*, 1999

Notes from a Lewis Carroll Meeting

Selwyn Goodacre (an eminent Carroll scholar) pointed out that the violence in the *Alice* books is tempered by the genius of Carroll: it is funny and controlled. He also noted that it is not a coincidence that children's books after *Alice* became known for higher-quality illustrations. During a speech to the Lewis Carroll Society of North America, Goodacre listed 10 ideas that Carroll pioneered in the art of children's literature.

1. the journey into strange lands
2. the quest for the golden garden (possibly because of the difficulty of getting into many of the gardens in Oxford)
3. the vehicle for humor (in general, there had not been much humor in children's books previous to *Alice*)
4. a message that included manners, independent minds and the ability to argue without being officious
5. an extemporaneous tale
6. a satire of contemporary life
7. instruction in logic and mathematics
8. language play
9. a nonsense story including anthropomorphic animals
10. a strong (female) character

—"The Lewis Carroll Centenary Program,"
Knight Letter, Autumn 1998

"ALICE IN WONDERLAND"

FEATURING CHARLOTTE HENRY AS "ALICE"

Lewis Carroll

THE BIG LITTLE BOOK

LIFE

Life Presents
THREE MODERN HOUSES
IN COLOR

CLASSICS Illustrated
NO. 49   25c
FEATURING STORIES BY THE WORLD'S GREATEST AUTHORS
ALICE in WONDERLAND
By Lewis Carroll

WALT DISNEY'S
Alice in Wonderland
A BIG GOLDEN BOOK

TV GUIDE
The wonders of **Alice**

The Collectible Alice

Despite the appropriation of the *Alice* books by academic literary culture, the *Alice* myth still informs popular culture in general. Both the *Wonderland* and *Looking-Glass* stories have been adapted for stage, ballet, opera, film and television, and have served as the bases for many advertising campaigns, including the now-famous Guinness advertisements of the 1920s and 30s. Numerous clubs and societies are devoted to *Alice* study and fandom, both in America and abroad. What Morton Cohen has labeled "the *Alice* industry" also continues to generate countless *Alice*-inspired commercial enterprises: collectibles from tee shirts to teapots, chess sets, postcards, thimbles, dolls, diaries, jewelry, clocks, figurines, music and music videos, comic books, puppet shows, cartoons, stage productions, and film adaptations ranging from musical comedies to soft-core pornography. This lucrative and popular "industry" responds to readers' desires, motivated originally by the marketing efforts of the author, to possess not only the books, but the mythos surrounding the books' heroine.

—Carolyn Sigler, *Alternative Alices*, 1997

LEFT: *Alice on the cover of* Life Magazine *(April 28, 1947); as a Classic Comic (1948); as re-imagined by Walt Disney from the 1950s; as five Madame Alexander "Alice" dolls dating from the 1930s to the 1970s; and as a made-for-TV movie starring Tina Majorina in 1999.*
ABOVE: *A promotional pamphlet for Yellowstone National Park from the early 1900s.*

229

"Come with me,"

said Alice, "I'll show you why

Ford's Out Front!"

from Charles L. Dodgson
to Beatrice Hatch

November 13, 1873

I met her just outside Tom Gate, walking very stiffly, and I think she was trying to find her way to my rooms. So I said, "Why have you come here without Birdie?" So she said, "Birdie's gone! And Emily's gone! And Mabel isn't kind to me!" And two little waxy tears came running down her cheeks.

Why, how stupid of me! I've never told you who it was, all the time! It was your new doll. I was very glad to see her, and I took her to my room, and gave her some Vesta matches to eat, and a cup of nice melted wax to drink, for the poor thing was <u>very</u> hungry and thirsty after her long walk. So I said, "Come and sit down by the fire, and let's have a comfortable chat." "Oh, no! <u>no</u>!" she said. "I'd <u>much</u> rather not! You know I do melt so very easily!" And she made me take her quite to the other side of the room, where it was very cold: and then she sat on my knee, and fanned herself with a penwiper, because she said she was afraid the end of her nose was beginning to melt.

"You've no *idea* how careful we have to be, we dolls," she said. "Why there was a sister of mine — would you believe it? — she went up to the fire to warm her hands, and one of her hands dropped right off! There now!"

"Of course it dropped *right* off," I said, "because it was the *right* hand."

"And how do you know it was the *right* hand, Mister Carroll?" the doll said.

So I said, "I think it must have been the right hand, because the other hand was *left*."

The doll said, "I shan't laugh. It's a very bad joke. Why, even a common wooden doll could make a better joke than that. And besides, they've made my mouth so stiff and hard, that I *can't* laugh, even if I try ever so much!"

Isa's Adventures in Oxford

CHAPTER I

On Wednesday, the Eleventh of July, Isa happened to meet a friend at Paddington Station at half-past ten. She can't remember his name, but she says he was an old, old gentleman, and he had invited her, she thinks to go with him somewhere or other, she can't remember where.

CHAPTER II

The first thing they did, after calling at a shop, was to go to the Panorama of the "Falls of Niagara." Isa thought it very wonderful. You seemed to be on the top of a tower, with miles and miles of country all round you. The things in front were real, and somehow they joined into the picture behind, so that you couldn't tell where the real things ended and the picture began.

After that Isa and her friend (A.A.M., the aged aged man) went to the house of a Mr. Dymes. Mrs. Dymes gave them some dinner, and two of her children, called Helen and Maud, went with them to Terry's Theatre, to see the play of "Little Lord Fauntleroy." Little Vera Beringer was the little Lord Fauntleroy. Isa would have liked to play the part, but the Manager at the Theatre did not allow her, as she did not know the words.

Then they all went off to the metropolitan Railway, and the two Miss

This story was handwritten by Lewis Carroll and sent to Isa Bowman following her visit to him in 1888. When Bowman wrote her memoir, *The Story of Lewis Carroll*, in 1900, she reprinted this story in Carroll's original handwriting. It has been edited for inclusion here.

Dymeses got off at their station, and Isa and the A.A.M. went on to Oxford. A kind old lady called Mrs. Symonds, had invited Isa to come and sleep at her house: and she was soon fast asleep, and dreaming that she and little Lord Fauntleroy were going in a steamer down the Falls at Niagara.

CHAPTER III

The next morning Isa set off, almost before she was awake, with the A.A.M., to pay a visit to a little college called Christ Church (built in 1546). You go in under a magnificent tower, called "Tom Tower," nearly four feet high (so that Isa had hardly to stoop at all to go under it) into the Great Quadrangle (which very vulgar people call "Tom Quad.") You should always be polite, even when speaking to a Quadrangle: it might seem not to take any notice, but it doesn't like being called names.

They had breakfast at Ch. Ch. (Christ Church), in the rooms of the A.A.M., and then Isa learned how to print with the "Typewriter," and printed several beautiful volumes of poetry, all of her own invention. By this time it was 1 o'clock so Isa paid a visit to the kitchen to make sure that the chicken, for her dinner, was being properly roasted.

Then they saw the dining hall in which the A.A.M. has dined several times (about 8000 times, perhaps). After dinner, they went

View of Oxford from a postcard dated 1903.

through the quadrangle of the Bodleian Library, into Broad Street, and, as a band was just going by, of course they followed it. (Isa likes Bands better than anything in the world, except Lands, and walking on Sands, and wringing her Hands.) The band led them into the gardens of Wadham College (built in 1613), where there was a school-treat going on. The treat was, first marching twice round the garden — then having a photograph done of them, all in a row — then a promise of "Punch and Judy," which wouldn't start for 20 minutes. So Isa, and Co., wouldn't wait, but went back to Ch. Ch. In the evening they played at "Reversi," till Isa had lost the small remainder of her temper. Then she went to bed, and dreamed she was Judy, and was beating Punch with a stick of barley sugar.

CHAPTER IV

On Friday morning (after taking her medicine very amiably), Isa went with the A.A.M. (who would go with her, though she told him over and over she would rather be alone) to the gardens of Worcester College (built in 1714) where they didn't see the swans (who ought to have been on the lake), nor the hippopotamus, who ought not to have been walking about among the flowers, gathering honey like a busy bee.

After breakfast Isa helped the A.A.M. to pack his luggage, because he thought he would go away, he didn't know where, some day, he didn't know when. So she put a lot of things, she didn't know what, into boxes, she didn't know which.

After dinner they went to St. John's College (built in 1555), and admired the Large Lawn, where more than 150 ladies, dressed in robes of gold and silver, were not walking about.

Then they saw the Chapel of Keble College (built in 1870): and then the New Museum, where Isa quite lost her heart to a charming stuffed Gorilla that smiled on her from a glass case.

CHAPTER V

On Saturday Isa had a music lesson and learned to play an American Orguinette. It is not a very difficult instrument to play, as you only have to turn a handle round and round: so she did it nicely. You put a long piece of paper in it, and it goes through the machine, and the holes in the paper make different notes play. They put one in the wrong end first, and had a tune backwards, and soon found themselves in the day before yesterday: so, they dared not go on, for fear of making Isa so young, she would not be able to talk.

In the afternoon they went into Magdalen Meadow, which has a pretty walk all round it, arched over with trees: and there they met a lady "from Amurrica," as she told them, who wanted to know the way to "Addison's Walk," and particularly wanted to know if there would be "any danger" in going there. They told her the way, and that most of the lions and tigers and buffaloes, round the meadow, were quite gentle and hardly ever killed people: so she set off, pale and trembling, and they saw her no more: only they heard her screams in the distance; so they guessed what had happened to her.

Then they rode in a tram-car to another part of Oxford, and called on a lady called Mrs. Jeane, and her little grand-daughter, called "Noel," because she was born on Christmas-day ("Noel" is the French name for "Christmas.") And there they had so much Tea that at last Isa nearly turned into a "Teaser."

Then they went home, down a little narrow street, where there was a

little dog standing fixed in the middle of the street, as if its feet were glued to the ground: they asked it how long it meant to stand there, and it said (as well as it could) "till the week after next."

Then Isa went to bed, and dreamed she was going round Magdalen Meadow, with the "Amurrican" lady and there was a buffalo sitting at the top of every tree, handing her cups of tea as she went underneath: but they all held the cups upside-down, so that the tea poured all over her head and ran down her face.

CHAPTER VI

On Sunday morning they went to St. Mary's church, in High Street. In coming home, down the street next to the one where they had found a fixed dog, they found a fixed cat — a poor little kitten, that had put out its head through the bars of the cellar-window, and couldn't get back out again. They rang the bell at the next door, but the maid said the cellar wasn't in that house, and, before they could get to the right door the cat had unfixed its head—either from its neck or from the bars—and had gone inside. Isa thought the animals in this city have a curious way of fixing themselves up and down the place as if they were hat-pegs.

In the middle of the day, as usual, Isa had her dinner: but this time it was grander than usual. There was a dish of "Meringues" (this is pronounced "Marangs"), which

Isa thought so good that she would have liked to live on them all the rest of her life.

They took a little walk in the afternoon. They saw "Mansfield College," a new college just begun to be built, with such tremendous narrow windows that Isa was afraid the young gentlemen who came there would not be able to see to learn their lessons, and would go away from Oxford just as wise as they came.

Then they went to the evening service at New College, and heard some beautiful singing and organ-playing. Then back to Ch. Ch., in pouring rain. Isa tried to count the drops, but when she had counted four million, three hundred and seventy-eight thousand, two hundred and forty-seven, she got tired of counting and left off.

After dinner Isa got somebody or other (she is not sure who it was), to finish this story for her. Then she went to bed, and dreamed she was fixed in the middle of Oxford, with her feet fast to the ground, and her head between the bars of a cellar-window, in a sort of final tableau. Then she dreamed the curtain came down, and the people all called out "Encore!" But she cried out, "Oh, not again! It would be too dreadful to have my visit all over again!" But, on second thought, she smiled in her sleep, and said "Well, do you know, after all, I think I wouldn't mind so very much if I did it all over again!"

The End

RIGHT: *Isa Bowman posing as Alice in Wonderland.*

A

is for
Alice

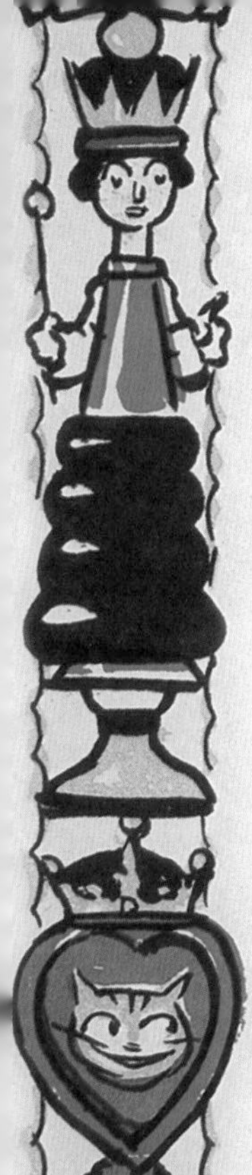

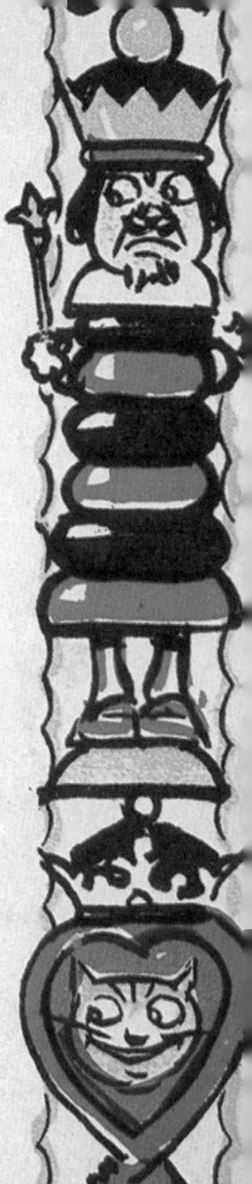

A is for Alice and all she
    went through
In Looking-glass land and
    in Wonderland, too.
How I wish I might go with
    dear little Alice
For a game of croquet at the
    Queen of Hearts' palace.

—Tony Sarg, *Tony Sarg's Alphabet*, n.d.

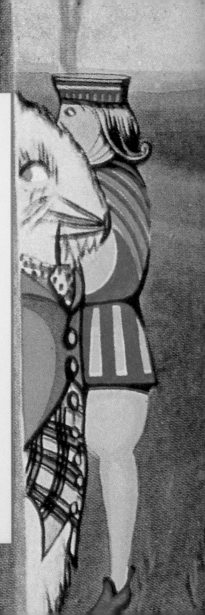

Did you ever play at Croquet?
There are large wooden balls, painted
with different colors, that you have to
roll about; and arches of wire, that you
have to send them through; and great
wooden mallets, with long handles, to
knock the balls about with.

—*The Nursery Alice*, 1890

"I know what you're thinking about," said Tweedledum; "but it isn't so, nohow."

"Contrariwise," continued Tweedledee, "if it was so, it might be; and if it were so, it would be; but as it isn't, it ain't. That's logic."

—*Through the Looking-Glass and What Alice Found There*, 1872

Closely related to Carroll's inversion humor is his humor of logical contradiction . . . He once wrote to his sister: "Please analyze logically the following piece of reasoning:

Little Girl: I'm *so* glad I don't like asparagus.
Friend: Why, my dear?
Little Girl: Because if I *did* like it, I should have to eat it—and I can't bear it!"

—Martin Gardner, *The Annotated Alice*, 2000

Do You Have a Perfectly Balanced Mind?

Take the two words "fuming" and "furious." Make up your mind that you will say both words, but leave it unsettled which you will say first. Now open your mouth and speak. If your thoughts incline ever so little towards "fuming," you will say "fuming-furious": if they turn, by even a hair's breadth, towards "furious," you will say "furious-fuming"; but if you have rarest of gifts, a perfectly balanced mind, you will say "frumious."

—*Rhyme? and Reason?*, 1895

Wonderland

Take a Bone From a Dog: What Remains to Be Seen?

Alice considered. "The bone wouldn't remain, of course, if I took it — and the dog wouldn't remain: it would come to bite me — and I'm sure I shouldn't remain!"

"Then you think nothing would remain?" said the Red Queen.

"I think that's the answer."

"Wrong, as usual," said the Red Queen: "the dog's temper would remain."

"But I don't see how—"

"Why, look here!" the Red Queen cried. "The dog would lose its temper, wouldn't it?"

"Perhaps it would," Alice replied cautiously.

"Then if the dog went away, its temper would remain!" the Queen exclaimed triumphantly.

—Through the Looking-Glass and What Alice Found There, 1872

251

Riddles from

Three sisters at breakfast
   were feeding the cat;
The first gave it sole—
   Puss was grateful for that:
The next gave it salmon—
   which Puss thought a treat:
The third gave it herring—
   which Puss wouldn't eat.
(Explain the conduct of the cat.)

SOLUTION:
   That salmon and sole Puss should think very grand
   Is no such remarkable thing.
   For more of these dainties Puss took up her stand;
   But when the third sister stretched out her fair hand
      Pray why should Puss swallow her ring?

—Lewis Carroll, *Puzzles from Wonderland*, 1870

Wonderland

Alice sighed wearily. "I think you might do something better with the time," she said, "than wasting it in asking riddles that have no answers."

"If you knew Time as well as I do," said the Hatter, "you wouldn't talk about wasting *it*. It's *him*."

"I don't know what you mean," said Alice.

"Of course you don't!" the Hatter said, tossing his head contemptuously. "I dare say you never even spoke to Time!"

—*Alice's Adventures in Wonderland,* 1865

Games and Tricks

The 30 Letter Game

Charles Dodgson invented this game in 1895 and recommended it for "light mental recreation."

1. Take 4 or 5 complete alphabets.
2. Put the vowels in one bag, the consonants in another.
3. Shake up.
4. Draw 9 vowels and 21 consonants.
5. With these, you must make 6 real words (excluding proper names) so as to use all the letters.

FOR TWO PLAYERS: Pick out the 30 letters as above and then pick out a set of duplicate letters. Sit apart from each other and see who finishes first.

SHORTER PLAY: Draw 6 vowels and 14 consonants and make 4 words.

EVEN SHORTER PLAY: Draw 3 vowels and 7 consonants and make 2 words.

from Wonderland

Magic Trick

1. Put handkerchief over your right hand.
2. Cross the front corners (A and B) and pull them up between your fingers.
3. Now the rabbit has ears. Tuck them tightly between your fingers (see picture.)
4. Stuff the ends of the handkerchief into your right sleeve, and put matchstick ends under the "ears" for eyes. Move your middle and ring fingers, and offer your rabbit a cookie!

1.

2.

3.

4.

Bob the Bat

There was another wonderful toy which he sometimes produced for me, and this was known as "The Bat." The ceilings of the rooms in which he lived at the time were very high indeed, and admirably suited for the purposes of "The Bat." It was an ingeniously constructed toy of gauze and wire, which actually flew about the room like a bat. It was worked by a piece of twisted elastic, and it could fly for about half a minute.

I was always a little afraid of this toy because it was too life-like, but there was a fearful joy in it. When the music-boxes began to pall he would get up from his chair and look at me with a knowing smile. I always knew what was coming even before he began to speak, and I used to dance up and down in tremendous anticipation.

"Isa, my darling," he would say, "once upon a time there was some-one called Bob the Bat! And he lived in the top left-hand drawer of the writing table. What could he do when uncle wound him up?"

And then I would squeak out breathlessly, "He could really Fly!"

Bob the Bat had many adventures. There was no way of controlling the direction of its flight, and one morning, a hot summer's morning when the window was wide open, Bob flew out into the garden and alighted in a bowl of salad which a scout was taking to someone's rooms. The poor fellow was so startled by the sudden flapping apparition that he dropped the bowl, and it was broken into a thousand pieces.

—Isa Bowman, *The Story of Lewis Carroll*, 1900

Puzzles from

Doublets

Just a year ago last Christmas, two young ladies—smarting under that sorest scourge of feminine humanity, the having "nothing to do"—besought me to send them "some riddles." But riddles I had none at hand, and therefore set myself to devise some other form of verbal torture which should serve the same purpose. The result of my meditations was a new kind of Puzzle—new at least to me—which, now that it had been fairly tested by a year's experience and commended by many friends, I offer to you.

The rules of the Puzzle are simple enough. Two words are proposed, of the same length; and the Puzzle consists of linking these together by interposing other words, each of which shall differ from the next word in one letter only. That is to say, one letter may be changed in one of the given words, then one letter in the next word, till we arrive at the given word. For example, here is how you would turn HEAD into TAIL.

HEAD
Heal
Teal
Tell
Tall
TAIL

I call the two given words "a Doublet," the interposed words are "links," and the entire series is a "Chain."

—*Vanity Fair*, March 24, 1879

260

Wonderland

T he game proved very popular and in subsequent issues, Carroll submitted many other
"Doublets." He later amended the game by
adding another rule that allowed a player, at any
step, to re-arrange the letters of a word, instead
of introducing a new letter (though you could not
do both at the same time.) For example, to turn
IRON into LEAD

IRON
Icon
Coin
Corn
Cord
Lord
Load
LEAD

Here are some for you to solve:

1. Drive PIG into STY
2. Raise FOUR to FIVE
3. Bring JACK to JILL
4. Evolve MAN from APE
5. Run COMB into HAIR

6. Make FLOUR into BREAD
7. Make BREAD into TOAST
8. Turn POOR to RICH
9. Change NOUN to VERB
10. Bring SHIP into DOCK

SOLUTIONS:

1.	2.	3.	4.	5.	6.	7.	8.	9.	10.
PIG	FOUR	JACK	APE	COMB	FLOUR	BREAD	POOR	NOUN	SHIP
Wig	Foul	Sack	Are	Come	Floor	Break	Boor	Noon	Slip
Wag	Fool	Sick	Ere	Home	Flood	Bleak	Book	Moon	Slap
Way	Foot	Silk	Err	Hole	Blood	Bleat	Rook	Morn	Soap
Say	Fort	Sill	Ear	Hale	Brood	Blest	Rock	More	Soak
STY	Fore	JILL	Mar	Hall	Broad	Blast	Rick	Mere	Sock
	Fire		MAN	Hail	BREAD	Boast	RICH	Here	DOCK
	FIVE			HAIR		TOAST		Herb	
								VERB	

261

Riddles from

John gave his brother James a box:
About it were many locks.

James woke and said it gave him pain;
So gave it back to John again.

The box was not with lid supplied.
Yet caused his lids to open wide:

And all these locks had never a key—
What kind of box, then, could it be?

SOLUTION:
As curly-headed James was sleeping in a bed,
His brother John gave him a blow on the head;
James opened his eyelids, and spying his brother,
Doubled his fist, and gave him another.
This kind of box then is not so rare;
The lids are eyelids, the locks are the hair,
And so every schoolboy can tell to his cost,
The key to the tangles is constantly lost.

—*Puzzles from Wonderland,* 1870

Wonderland

Dreaming of apples on a wall,
And dreaming often, dear,
I dreamed that, if I counted all,
—How many would appear?

SOLUTION:

If **ten** the number
dreamed **of**,* why
'tis clear

That in the dream ten
apples would appear.

—*Puzzles from Wonderland*, 1870

*Editor's note: as in of-ten

"Who cares for you?" said Alice (she had grown to her full size by this time). "You're nothing but a pack of cards!"

—*Alice's Adventures in Wonderland*, 1865

UN-DISH THE FISH

"First, the fish must be caught."
That is easy: a baby, I think, could have caught it.
"Next, the fish must be bought."
That is easy: a penny, I think, would have bought it.

"Now cook me the fish!"
That is easy, and will not take more than a minute.
"Let it lie in a dish!"
That is easy, because it already is in it.

"Bring it here! Let me sup!"
It is easy to set such a dish on the table.
"Take the dish-cover up!"
Ah, THAT is so hard that I fear I'm unable!

For it holds it like glue—
Holds the lid to the dish, while it lies in the middle:
Which is easiest to do,
Un-dish-cover the fish, or dishcover the riddle?

—Through the Looking-Glass and What Alice Found There, 1872

THE QUEEN OF HEARTS' STRAWBERRY JAM TARTS

3 cups strawberries, cut up
1 cup sugar
1/2 cup water
2 envelopes Knox unflavored gelatin
4 4" pie crust pastry shells, pre-baked
Devon Cream

Bring strawberries, sugar, and water to a boil in a 1-quart saucepan. Turn down heat and sprinkle the gelatin evenly over the berry mixture while stirring constantly. Bring mixture back to boiling for 5 minutes, stir frequently. Allow mixture to cool until it stops steaming. Pour mixture into baked tart shells. Cool and serve topped with a dollop of Devon Cream.

But I was thinking of a way
   To feed oneself on batter.
And so go on from day to day
   Getting a little fatter.

—*Through the Looking-Glass and
What Alice Found There*, 1872

270

The White Queen's Rules

1 The rule is, jam to-morrow and jam yesterday — but never jam today. 2 It's jam every other day: to-day isn't any other day.

3 It's a poor sort of memory that only works backwards. 4 The effect of living backwards always makes one a little giddy at first—but there's one great advantage in it, that one's memory works both ways. 5 Nobody can do two things at once.

—Through the Looking-Glass and What Alice Found There, 1872

ORANGE MARMALADE NOODLE PUDDING

1 pound noodles
4 ounces butter
1 cup sugar
4 eggs
$1/2$ pound cottage cheese
1 pint sour cream
$1/2$ cup milk
2 apples (peeled, cored, diced)
1 small can peaches
   (drain syrup)
1 tsp. vanilla
$1/2$ jar orange marmalade
$1/2$ cup raisins
$1/2$ cup cornflakes
2 tbsp. cinnamon sugar

Preheat oven to 350°F. Parboil noodles (5 minutes) in 4 quarts of salted water and drain. Melt butter over noodles, making sure all noodles are drenched in butter. Mix sugar and eggs with an electric blender. Add cheese, sour cream and milk. Fold in apples, peaches, vanilla, marmalade and raisins. Add mixture to noodles and blend. Pour everything into a large glass baking dish. Fill dish $1/2$ to rim, allowing space for pudding to rise. Lightly sprinkle crushed cornflakes over top of pudding. Dot with butter and cinnamon sugar. Bake for one hour. Can be frozen and reheated.

HOW TO COOK A JUBJUB BIRD

You boil it in sawdust;
you salt it in glue:

You condense it with
locusts and tape:

Still keeping one principal
object in view —

To preserve its
symmetrical shape.

—The Hunting of the Snark, 1876

276

DRINK ME: PINK FLAMINGO LEMONADE

12 lemons
1/2 cup sugar
2 quarts water
8 oz. grenadine
Ice

Zest half of one lemon before juicing and set aside. Juice the 12 lemons and pour into a pitcher. Add the sugar, water and the grenadine. Add the lemon zest to the mixture and mix well. Add the ice and let melt for about 15 minutes. *Enjoy!*

If all the world were apple pie,
And all the sea were ink,
And all the trees were bread and cheese,
What *should* we have to drink?

—*The Rectory Umbrella*, c. 1849–50

Tripping Out

And that's only the beginning. When you take something that tastes like cherry tarts, custard, pineapple, roast turkey, toffee and toast at the same time and makes you grow and shrink—baby, that's tripping out.

—Thomas Fensch, *Alice in Acidland*, 1970

Good-bye Feet!

—Alice's Adventures in Wonderland, 1865

from Charles L. Dodgson
to Gertrude Chataway

October 13, 1875

I am writing this to wish you many and many a happy return of your birthday tomorrow. I will drink your health, if only I can remember, and if you don't mind—but perhaps you object? You see, if I were to sit by you at breakfast, and to drink your tea, you wouldn't like that, would you? You would say, "Boo! hoo! Here's Mr. Dodgson's drunk all my tea, and I haven't got any left!" So I am very much afraid, next time Sybil looks for you, she'll find you sitting by the sad sea wave, and crying, "Boo! hoo! Here's Mr. Dodgson has drunk my health, and I haven't got any left!" And how it will puzzle Dr. Maund, when he is sent for to see you! "My dear Madam, I'm very sorry to say your little girl has got <u>no health at all!</u> I never saw such a thing in my life!" "Oh, I can easily explain it!" your Mother will say. "You see she <u>would</u> go and make friends with a strange gentleman, and yesterday he drank her health!" "Well, Mrs. Chataway," he will say, "the only way to cure her is to wait till his next birthday, and then for <u>her</u> to drink his <u>health</u>"

WHITE RABBIT CARROT CAKE

3 cups flour
2$\frac{1}{2}$ cups sugar
1 tbsp. baking soda
1 tbsp. cinnamon
1 tsp. salt
4 eggs
1$\frac{1}{2}$ cups vegetable oil
1 tsp. vanilla
2 cups shredded carrots
8 oz. chopped walnuts
1 (15-oz.) can chopped
   pineapple

Preheat oven to 350°F. Grease and flour two round 9-inch cake pans. In large bowl mix flour, sugar, baking soda, cinnamon and salt. In large bowl, beat the eggs and add oil and vanilla.

Stir carrots, walnuts and pineapple into egg mixture. Add flour mixture into egg mixture and stir with a fork until flour is well moistened. Pour batter into pans and bake for 40 to 45 minutes at 350°. Allow to cool then remove from pans and frost.

CREAM CHEESE FROSTING
16 oz. cream cheese, at room
   temperature
8 oz. unsalted butter, at room
   temperature
1 tsp. vanilla
16 oz. powdered sugar, sifted

In a large bowl, beat until fluffy.

"**Y**ou don't know how to manage Looking-glass cakes," the Unicorn remarked. "Hand it round first, and cut it afterwards."

This sounded nonsense, but Alice very obediently got up, and carried the dish round, and the cake divided itself into three pieces as she did so. "*Now* cut it up," said the Lion, as she returned to her place with the empty dish.

—*Through the Looking-Glass and What Alice Found There*, 1872

THE MAD HATTER BREAD ROLLS

*Bread and butter is fine, but these sweet logs,
made from white bread, are much tastier!*

8 slices white bread
1 8-oz. package cream cheese
1 tsp. vanilla
1 egg yolk
2 tbsp. sugar
1/4 lb. sweet butter, melted
1 cup sugar
1 tsp. cinnamon
1 pint sour cream

Preheat oven to 350ºF. Remove crust from bread and roll bread thin. Blend together cream cheese, vanilla, egg yolk and 2 tbsp. sugar. Spread mixture on bread and roll into a log. Dip the log into the melted butter and roll in 1 cup sugar mixed with the cinnamon. Cut each log into 3 pieces and put on a cookie sheet. (At this point, you can freeze the logs. When you want to serve, thaw for 10 minutes before baking.) Bake for 10 minutes. Serve with sour cream for dipping.

288

WHAT FOOD DOES TO YOU

Pepper makes people
hot-tempered.

Vinegar makes them **sour**.

Chamomile makes them **bitter**.

Barley-sugar and such things
make children **sweet**-tempered.

—Alice's Adventures in Wonderland, 1865

291

RED PEPPER SOUP

6 red peppers
1 medium onion, chopped
2 cups celery, chopped
3 or 4 cloves garlic
8 cups chicken or vegetable broth
Chili peppers (optional)

Roast red peppers in hot oven (400°F) for 40 to 50 minutes, rotating often. Remove from oven, place in plastic bag till cool. Remove peel and seeds and set aside. Sauté onions, celery and garlic until tender. Add peppers and broth to cover. Simmer 15 to 20 minutes to blend flavors.

"There's certainly too much pepper in that soup!" Alice said to herself, as well as she could for sneezing.

—*Alice's Adventures in Wonderland*, 1865

Add chili peppers to taste. (Go easy, they're spicy!) Purée in blender or with a hand blender in pot. Simmer a little longer.

Boil it so easily.
Mix it so greasily.
Stir it so sneezily,
One! Two! Three!

—Lewis Carroll, written for the Cook for
the stage production of *Alice*, 1886

THE CHESHIRE CAT CHEESE STRAW WHISKERS

1 17^1/4-oz. package frozen puff pastry, thawed
^{3}/4 cup freshly grated Parmesan cheese
2 teaspoons cayenne pepper

Preheat the oven to 400°F. On a lightly floured work surface, place one sheet of the puff pastry (unfolded). Sprinkle ^{1}/4 cup of the cheese over the bottom half of the sheet, leaving a ^{1}/4-inch border along the edges. Sprinkle half the cayenne pepper over the cheese. Fold the pastry sheet with no cheese over the other half and sprinkle 2 more tablespoons of the cheese over the top. With a floured rolling pin, roll out the pastry to a 14 x 7-inch rectangle. Using a sharp knife, cut the pastry into ^{1}/2-inch strips. Twist each strip several times and place them an inch apart on heavy ungreased baking sheets, gently pressing down on the ends of each strip to keep it twisted. Bake for 11 to 13 minutes, or until golden brown. Let the straw whiskers cool on the pan for about 2 minutes. Using a wide spatula, transfer to wire racks to cool completely. Repeat with the remaining ingredients.

HINTS FOR ETIQUETTE; OR, DINING OUT MADE EASY

In proceeding to the dining room, the gentleman gives one arm to the lady he escorts—it is unusual to offer both.

To use a fork with your soup, intimating at the same time to your hostess that you are reserving the spoon for the beefsteaks, is a practice wholly exploded.

It is always allowable to ask for artichoke jelly with your boiled venison; however, there are houses where this is not supplied.

The method of helping roast turkey with two carving-forks is practicable, but deficient in grace.

We do not recommend the practice of eating cheese with a knife and fork in one hand, and a spoon and wine-glass in the other; there is a kind of awkwardness in the action which no amount of practice can entirely dispel.

As a general rule, do not kick the shins of the opposite gentleman under the table, if personally unacquainted with him; your pleasantry is liable to be misunderstood—a circumstance at all times unpleasant.

—Lewis Carroll, 1849

HUMPTY DUMPTY SCRAMBLED EGGS

2 tbsp. butter
1 small onion, chopped
4 eggs
4 oz. cream cheese, cut in $1/2$-inch cubes
1 tbsp. fresh chives, cut with scissors
Salt and white pepper to taste

Melt butter in a frying pan and add chopped onion. Sauté until light brown. Beat eggs well and add to onions. Add the cream cheese. Turn heat down to medium. Add chives and season with salt and pepper. Stir, scraping bottom of pan. Do not brown. *Serve hot!*

"I *have* tasted eggs, certainly," said Alice, who was a very truthful child; "but little girls eat eggs quite as much as serpents do, you know."

—*Alice's Adventures in Wonderland*, 1865

Humpty Dumpty

There he lay, stretched out on the ground,
While all the company gathered around;
When, valiantly stifling his tears and groans,
He sadly addressed them in quavering tones,

"Friends," said Humpty, wiping his eyes,
"This sudden descent was an awful surprise,
It inclines me to think—you may laugh at my views,—
That a seat that is humble is safest to choose."

"All are not fitted to sit on a wall,
Some have no balance, and some are too small;
Many have tried it and found, as I guess,
They've ended, like me, in a terrible mess."

"Hark, you horses, and all you king's men!
Hear it, and never forget it again!
'Tis those who are patient in seats that are low,
Who some day get up in high places and crow."

Then they took him and put him to bed.
I hope you'll remember the things that he said;
For all the king's horses and all the king's men
Never once thought of his sermon again.

—Anna Marion Smith, *St. Nicholas*, 1907

"All are not fitted to sit on a wall,
Some have no balance, and some are too small;
Many have tried it and found, as I guess,
They've ended, like me, in a terrible mess."

MOCK TURTLE PIE

CRUST
1 1/2 cups crushed chocolate
   cookies
1/2 cup melted butter

FILLING
3/4 cup hot fudge sauce
1 quart vanilla ice cream
1/2 cup butterscotch topping
8 pecan halves
1/4 cup whipping cream,
   sweetened and whipped

Preheat oven to 350°F. To prepare crust, mix cookie crumbs with butter. With the back of a spoon, press mixture into the bottom and up the sides of a 9-inch pie plate. Bake for 8 minutes, remove to wire rack and cool completely. Freeze. Spread 1/2 cup fudge sauce on the bottom of the prepared frozen pie shell. Freeze. Spade thin sheets of ice cream on top of fudge. Smooth and slightly mound ice cream in center of pan. Using the remainder of the hot fudge sauce, make a border around the edge of pan with a spoon. Drizzle butterscotch topping over ice cream and position pecan halves so that each slice will have a pecan in its center. Place whipped cream in a spiral-shaped mound in the center of the pie. Freeze until ready to serve.

THE OWL AND THE PANTHER

I passed by his garden, and
   marked, with one eye,
How the Owl and the Panther
   were sharing a pie:
The Panther took pie crust,
   gravy and meat.
While the Owl had the dish as
   its share of the treat.
When the pie was all finished,
   the Owl, as a boon,
Was kindly permitted to pocket
   the spoon.

—Alice's Adventures in Wonderland, 1865

BEAUTIFUL SOUP, SO RICH AND GREEN!

1 (16 oz.) package of dried green split peas
5 (13 oz.) cans of chicken broth
1 bay leaf
1 medium onion, chopped
1 cup of carrots, peeled and sliced thick
6 stalks of celery, chopped
1 yellow pepper, chopped
Salt and pepper to taste

Rinse peas in cool water. Put peas, chicken broth and bay leaf in a pot and bring to a boil. Lower heat and simmer for 20 minutes. Add onion, carrots, celery and yellow pepper. Cover partially and simmer for about an hour. Stir occasionally. Add water if soup becomes too thick. Add salt and pepper.

Beautiful Soup, so rich and green,
Waiting in a hot tureen!
Who for such dainties would not stoop?
Soup of the evening, beautiful Soup!
Soup of the evening, beautiful Soup!

—*Alice's Adventures in Wonderland,* 1865

LOBSTER QUADRILLE

'Tis the voice of the Lobster; I heard him declare

"You have baked me too brown,
I must sugar my hair."

As a duck with its eyelids, so he
with his nose

Trims his belt and his buttons,
and turns out his toes.

When the sands are all dry, he is
gay as a lark,

And will talk in contemptuous
tones of the Shark:

But, when the tide rises and
sharks are around,

His voice has a timid and tremulous sound.

—*Alice's Adventures in Wonderland*, 1865

309

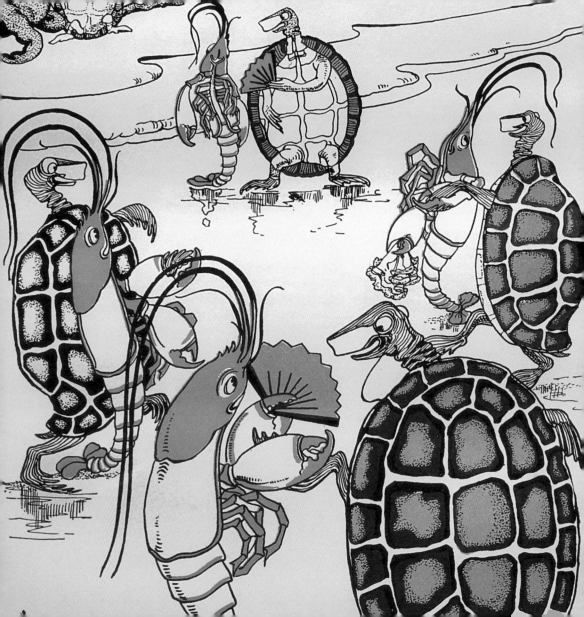

Fond of Fishes

"Do you know, I've had such a quantity of poetry repeated to me to-day," Alice began, a little frightened at finding that, the moment she opened her lips, there was dead silence, and all eyes were fixed upon her; "and it's a very curious thing, I think—every poem was about fishes in some way. Do you know why they're so fond of fishes, all about here?"

—*Through the Looking-Glass and What Alice Found There*, 1872

Change Lobsters and Dance

"What sort of a dance is it?" [asked Alice.]

"Why," said the Gryphon, "you first form into a line along the sea shore—"

"Two lines!" cried the Mock Turtle. "Seals, turtles, salmon and so on: then, when you've cleared all the jelly-fish out of the way—"

"That generally takes some time," interrupted the Gryphon.

"—you advance twice—"

"Each with a lobster as a partner!" cried the Gryphon.

—*Alice's Adventures in Wonderland*, 1865

A World of Nonsense

What can I really manage to remember of my early readings and re-readings of the *Alice* books?

. . . I remember—though how I should have put it into words as a child I do not know—that this was a book about working out who you were. About identity, constant and threatened. I was pleasantly frightened by Alice's changes of size, by her chin hitting her feet, which I thought was dreadfully funny, by her growing as large as the house she was in, by her long-necked peering into the nest of the pigeon who disconcertingly categorized her as a serpent. I am now fairly certain that this sense of fluid size and identity feels very different to children from how it appears to adults. Children are in fact always changing size, and many of them seem to believe, as my own son did, that adults get smaller and younger as children get larger and older. It is not really to do with puberty or sexual maturity, as many interpretations of *Alice* have argued. It is about something earlier, more primitive than that. You have only to think of the pleasures of fairy tales—the anticipation of Love, the fulfillment of wishes, the punishment of evil—to realize how very different the world of *Alice* is. It is a world in which odd lessons are learned and odd rules are perceived, by trial and error, to exist—quite safely, because this is a world of nonsense.

—A. S. Byatt, Introduction,
Alice's Adventures in Wonderland, 2002

Child with Dreaming Eyes

"Alice," Child with
  dreaming eyes,
Noting things that
  come to pass
Turvey-wise in
  Wonderland
Backwards through a
  Looking-Glass

—The Westminster Alice, Saki
(Hector Hugo Munro), 1900

Rules of Battle

I. If one Knight hits the other, he knocks him off his horse; if he misses, he tumbles off himself.

II. They hold their clubs with their arms, as if they are Punch and Judy.

III. They always fall on their heads.

IV. The battle ends with their both falling off in this way, side by side.

V. When they get up again, they shake hands.

—*Through the Looking-Glass and What Alice Found There,* 1872

Farewell

Of all the episodes the most unforgettable one is the White Knight's farewell. Perhaps in that moment the Knight is deeply touched because he cannot anymore ignore that he is only a dream of Alice's, as she herself is a dream of the Red King, and that he is at the point of vanishing. At the same time, the Knight is Lewis Carroll who says goodbye to the beloved dreams that filled his solitude.

—Jorge Luis Borges, translated by Immo C. Günzerodt, *Knight Letter 55*, Summer 1997

316

All this she took in like a picture . . . watching the strange pair, and listening, in a half-dream, to the melancholy music of the song.

—*Through the Looking-Glass and What Alice Found There*, 1872

Adults & Children

Alice in Wonderland is, in effect, two books: a book for children and a book for adults. Its interest, its fantasy, its humor and its logic all operate at two levels. I know that adults often wonder why and how Alice can appeal to children. I suspect that children wonder why adults like it ...

Perhaps adults also love *Alice* for a deeper and more important reason. Most adults, most successful adults, most happy adults, never really or quite stop being children.

—Warren Weaver, *Alice in Many Tongues*, 1964

Let us once more adventure, hand in hand:
Give me belief again—in Wonderland!

—Vincent Starrett, "Brillig," 1949

The last level of metaphor in the *Alice* books is this: that life, viewed rationally and without illusion, appears to be a nonsense tale told by an idiot mathematician.

—Martin Gardner, Introduction,
The Annotated Alice, 2000

VISITING WC

Wouldn't it be a nice thing
to have a **curious dream**,
just like Alice? The best plan is
this. First lie down under a tree,
and **wait** till a White Rabbit runs
by, with a watch in his hand: then
shut your eyes, and **pretend**
to be dear little Alice.

—*The Nursery Alice, 1890*

ONDERLAND

"Oh, I've had such a curious dream!" said Alice. And she told her sister, as well as she could remember them, all these strange Adventures of hers that you have just been reading about; and, when she had finished, her sister kissed her, and said, "It *was* a curious dream, dear, certainly; but now run in to your tea: it's getting late." So Alice got up and ran off, thinking while she ran, as well she might, what a wonderful dream it had been.

—*Alice's Adventures in Wonderland*, 1865

324

"Is Life itself
a dream,
I wonder?"
—*Sylvie and Bruno, 1889*

APPENDIX

Alice in Film & Television

1903 *Alice in Wonderland* Silent. U.K. Produced by Cecil Hepworth. Alice: May Clark. The first Alice movie features sixteen scenes and runs ten minutes.

1910 *Alice in Wonderland* Silent. U.S. Edison Manufacturing Company. Filmed in the Bronx, the film is a one-reeler which runs for ten minutes.

1915 *Alice in Wonderland* Silent. U.S. Nonpareil Feature Film Company.

It's easy to see
You don't need a palace
To feel like Alice
In Wonderland

—Johnny Mercer and Harry Warren, "On the Atchison, Topeka and The Santa Fe," *The Harvey Girls*, 1945

Filmed on an estate in Long Island, the film also contains scenes from *Looking-Glass* and runs for fifty minutes.

1931 *Alice in Wonderland* U.S. Commonwealth Pictures. The first "talkie" starred Ruth Gilbert as Alice.

1933 *Alice in Wonderland* U.S. Paramount Productions. The film, with Charlotte Henry as Alice and a star-studded cast including W. C. Fields, Edna May Oliver, Cary Grant and Gary Cooper, had advanced visual effects for its time. It has never been commercially released, although an abbreviated version has occasionally been broadcast on television.

1948 *Alice in Wonderland* France. A Lou Bunin film. Most of the characters, except for Alice (Carol Marsh), are puppets. Walt Disney tried to stop distribution of

328

"For it might end, you know," said Alice to herself, "in my going out altogether, like a candle. I wonder what I should be like then?" And she tried to fancy what the flame of a candle looks like after the candle is blown out, for she could not remember ever having seen such a thing.

—*Alice's Adventures in Wonderland*, 1865

In true *Through the Looking-Glass* fashion, the career of Charlotte Henry (*background photo*) started with a leading role as Alice in Paramount's 1933 *Alice in Wonderland*, spiraled into lesser parts, and then evaporated altogether.

With an all-star cast including W. C. Fields as Humpty Dumpty, Edna May Oliver as the Red Queen, Cary Grant as the Mock Turtle and Gary Cooper as the White Knight, the 1933 film *Alice in Wonderland* did much to advance visual effects for its time and some critics call it the best film version of the book yet made. But the public did not agree. The film has fallen into obscurity and is not legally available for rental (although bootleg copies can be found on the Internet). Perhaps one of the reasons that the film tanked was because its stars were so heavily costumed they were not even recognizable, as is apparent in this still from the Tea Party scene.

this film in the U.S. as he perceived it as competition for his version.

1951 *Alice in Wonderland* U.S. A Walt Disney animated film with Kathryn Beaumont as the voice of (and model for) Alice. The film was poorly received when it opened but has become more and more popular over the years.

1954 "Alice in Wonderland," New Hallmark Hall of Fame. U.K. TV special.

1965 "Alice" U.K. teleplay by Dennis Potter, used later as a basis for *Dreamchild*.

1966 "What's a Nice Kid Like You Doing in a Place Like This," Hanna-Barbera. U.S. Animated TV production with Bill Dana, Sammy Davis Jr. and Zsa Zsa Gabor.

1966 "Alice Through the Looking-Glass" U.S. television broadcast, with Jimmy Durante, the Smothers Brothers and Ricardo Montalban.

1966 "Alice in Wonderland" U.K. BBC television, directed by Jonathan Miller. A dark, surreal portrayal, with Sir John Gielgud, Sir Michael Redgrave and Peter Sellers. There were no special effects or animal costumes.

1972 "Alice's Adventures in Wonderland" U.K. Musical starring Fiona Fullerton, Peter Sellers, Dudley Moore and Spike Milligan.

1981 "Alice at the Palace" U.S. A musical version with Meryl Streep.

1983 "Alice in Wonderland" U.S. television broadcast of Eva Le Gallienne's 1931 stage version, this time with Broadway's brightest lights (Richard Burton, Nathan Lane, etc.).

1985 *Dreamchild* U.K. Dennis Potter's brilliant story inspired by Alice Liddell Hargreaves's visit to the U.S. in 1932.

1985 "Alice in Wonderland/Through the Looking-Glass" U.S. A two-part television miniseries by Irwin Allen, with a cast of stars that included everyone you've ever heard of and, for once, an Alice under the age of ten.

1991 *Alice* Czechoslovakia. Jan Svankmajer's brilliant, if flawed, mixture of live action and stop-motion animation.

1999 "Alice Through the Looking-Glass" U.K. television production with Kate Beckinsale.

1999 "Alice in Wonderland" U.K./U.S. A dour Alice (Tina Majorino) in a way off-base three-hour made-for-TV production saved only by its amazing digital effects. Starring Whoopi Goldberg, Martin Short, Peter Ustinov, Christopher Lloyd.

2000 "Alice Underground" U.S. Robert Lee's photographic adaptation of Alice's trip through underground New York.

Mrs. Miniver (1942)

In the scene where the Miniver family huddles together in their bomb shelter during an air raid, Mrs. Miniver (Greer Garson) reads her children to sleep with *Alice in Wonderland*. After the children are asleep, she rereads one of the seminal passages in the book to her husband (Walter Pidgeon).

". . . and how she would keep, through all her riper years, the simple and loving heart of her childhood: and how she would gather about her other little children, and make their eyes bright and eager with many a strange tale, perhaps even with the dream of Wonderland of long ago: and how she would feel with all their simple sorrows, and find a pleasure in all their simple joys, remembering her own child-life, and the happy summer days."

333

Lewis Carroll Societies

The Lewis Carroll Society of North America (LCSNA)

The Lewis Carroll Society of North America (LCSNA), founded in 1974, is an organization of Carroll enthusiasts of all ages and backgrounds. Members come from throughout the world, with interests in virtually all of Lewis Carroll's many pursuits and in his continuing effect on our culture.

The society meets twice a year: in the spring and fall. Meeting places have included universities and libraries on both coasts and in between, with speakers such as Morton Cohen, Joyce Carol Oates, David Del Tredici and Douglas Hofstadter.

The LCSNA maintains a very active publications program. Members are automatically subscribed to the *Knight Letter* (a magazine with an artful blend of substantive, academic and lighter articles). The LCSNA has published more than a dozen books, including a multivolume series of Lewis Carroll pamphlets. The LCSNA also maintains the Lewis Carroll Home Page on their website: www.lewiscarroll.org. For more information, contact the secretary, Cindy Watter, P.O. Box 204, Napa CA 94559, U.S.A.; hedgehogccw@sbcglobal.net.

The Lewis Carroll Society (LCS) England

Founded in 1969 in England, the Lewis Carroll Society has more than 350 members and more than 40 institutional members, mostly from the United Kingdom but also from Japan, Australia, the United States, Canada and places as far away as Israel and Uruguay.

The Society publishes a wide range of books and pamphlets on various aspects of the author's life and work including the multivolume diaries of Lewis Carroll, edited by the eminent scholar Edward Wakeling. It also publishes several periodicals including *The Carrollian* (formerly called *Jabberwocky*); *The Lewis Carroll Review,* which provides informative reviews of Carroll-related books, exhibitions, films and theater productions; and, finally, *Bandersnatch,* a newsletter reporting on activities and Carrollian news generally.

Information about the Society and their publications can be found on www.lewiscarrollsociety.org.uk or by contacting The Secretary, 69 Cromwell Road, Hertford, Herts, SG13 7DP U.K.

The Daresbury Lewis Carroll Society

Founded in 1970, the Daresbury society consists of about 30 members in the North-West of England and is intended for those living in the area. For information about the Daresbury Society contact Mr. Kenn Outram, Blue Grass, Little Leigh, Northwich, Cheshire CW8 4RJ, U.K.

The Lewis Carroll Society of Canada (LCSC)

The LCSC was founded in 1996 and has about 60 members. Meetings in Canada are held twice a year and usually consist of three presentations followed by a social time. The Society's newsletter is called *White Rabbit Tales* and is published four times a year. The Society also publishes an annual booklet on a Carroll-related topic. Contact Dayna McCausland, Box 321, Erin, Ontario, N0B 1T0, Canada.

The Lewis Carroll Society of Japan (LCSJ)

The works of Lewis Carroll are enormously popular in Japan where more than 60 editions of *Alice in Wonderland* are currently in print. The society, founded in 1994, consists of approximately 170 members and publishes *Mischmasch*, an annual magazine written mainly in Japanese but with some in English. For more information contact The Lewis Carroll Society of Japan, University of Tsukuba, 1-1-1 Tennodai, Tsukuba, Ibaraki, 300-8571, Japan.

The Lewis Carroll Society of Australia (LCSA)

Founded in 1996, the LCS of Australia has about 35 members and, twice a year, publishes *The Lobster's Voice*, with information and entertaining pieces. (Contributions to the publication are always welcome.) Meetings are held twice a year. Contact The Lewis Carroll Society of Australia, 39 Sackville Street, Bexley, NSW 2207, Australia.

335

Alice in Cyberspace

(Sites are all live as of November 2003)

LEWIS CARROLL

www.lewiscarroll.org/carroll.html
The primary site for information, the "Lewis Carroll Home Page" is maintained by the Lewis Carroll Society of North America (*page 334*). You will find links to academic studies, biographies, bibliographies, teaching aids, texts, logic and mathematical works, games and puzzles, photography, sightings in popular culture and the media, things to buy, parodies, illustrators, critical analyses, lists of reference books, Carroll contacts, the 121 languages into which the Alice books have been translated and much, much more.

www.scholars.nus.edu.sg/victorian/authors/carroll/carrollov.html
The Victorian Web's page about Carroll has an academic orientation, with links to biography, religion, science, social and political history, his literary relations, genre, themes and other scholarly musings.

www.alice-in-wonderland.net   A friendly site in the Netherlands includes the script from the Disney movie, the original artwork that inspired Tenniel, originals of the poems that Carroll parodied and so forth.

www.aliceinoxford.net/index.htm
A good portal to the real Alice and Dodgson's lives in Oxford.

www.lookingforlewiscarroll.com/
"Contrariwise," a group of scholars who have "revisionist" views of Dodgson, have created an in-depth look at his life, his loves, his ideas and his works.

TEXTS

promo.net/pg/ The original Project Gutenberg text, hypertext, Acrobat and other formats for the major works can be found by typing "Carroll, Lewis" in the "author" search box.

www.bootlegbooks.com/fiction/Caroll/CompleteWorks/
As close to the complete works as any one site has.

www.hoboes.com/html/FireBlade/Carroll/Alice/Under/
Alice's Adventures under Ground, the precursor to *Wonderland*.

home.earthlink.net/~lfdean/carroll/ A few works not found in the above.

336

www.the-office.com/bedtime-story/classics-alice-1.htm
Wonderland is embellished with the works of nine classic (and two contemporary) illustrators.
megabrands.com/alice/indexx.html
The multimedia "Dynamic Text" version with music and simple animations. Has also a link to "Secrets of Lewis Carroll Revealed," which has some interesting analyses.
wiredforbooks.org/alice/ RealAudio version.
www.online-literature.com/carroll/alice/ A concordance to *Wonderland*.

MEDIA

www.alice-in-wonderland.fsnet.co.uk/ Magnificent site comprehensively detailing Alice in the movies, television, theater, audio recordings and so on.
www.helsinki.fi/~mlang/lewis/carroll-music.html
Music compositions inspired by Carroll.

SOCIETIES

www.lewiscarroll.org The Lewis Carroll Society of North America meets twice a year, publishes the *Knight Letter*, has outstanding publications and outreach programs and maintains the Lewis Carroll Home Page.
lewiscarrollsociety.org.uk The first of the Lewis Carroll Societies, founded in England, publishes three important serials. Their site is particularly strong on Dodgson's life and his Oxford milieu. An index of past articles from their publications also can be found on their site.

PHOTOGRAPHY

libserv3.princeton.edu/rbsc2/portfolio/lc-all-list.html The images of Dodgson's photographs in the Princeton collection, all in superb detail.
wsrv.clas.virginia.edu/~bhs2u/carroll/dodgson.html Two dozen of Dodgson's better known photographs, scanned from a book.

337

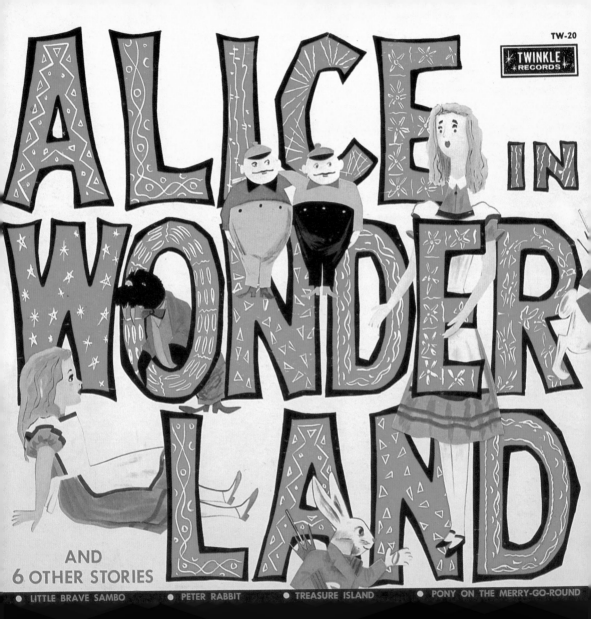

TW-20

TWINKLE
RECORDS

ALICE IN WONDERLAND

AND 6 OTHER STORIES

● LITTLE BRAVE SAMBO ● PETER RABBIT ● TREASURE ISLAND ● PONY ON THE MERRY-GO-ROUND

Alice in Cyberspace

PARODIES
www76.pair.com/keithlim/jabberwocky/parodies/ Links to many
Jabberwocky parodies: computers, politics, chemical elements and so on.

THINGS TO BUY
collectalice.home.att.net Link up with other Alice collectors.
www.sheepshop.com Buy directly from the "Sheep Shop" at Oxford,
depicted in *Through the Looking-Glass*, Chapter V: "Wool and Water."
www.wonderland.co.uk
A shop in Llandudno, North Wales, has a great selection.
www.thewhiterabbit.com A shop in Carmel, California.
www.bookstallsf.com/alice.html Always has delightful books.
www.wolfiewocky.com Collectibles, and an enormously large list of links (with
a high gibberish factor).

DISCUSSION GROUPS
groups.yahoo.com/group/lewiscarroll The only active and important discussion group.
mb.sparknotes.com/mb.epl?b=396 High school level.
www.lcsnz.org The Lewis Carroll Society of New Zealand has a "forum."

PORTALS IN OTHER LANGUAGES
The "Non-English" link on the Lewis Carroll Home Page has many dozen links.
Some particularly fine portal sites are:
German: *www.kidlane.lu/01inhalt/ereignisse/04_april/16/1865_alice_im_
wunderland/links.html*
Spanish: *mural.uv.es/jorgon/alicia.htm* and *www.expreso.co.cr/alicia*
French: *ibelgique.ifrance.com/carroll/*
Italian: *www.geocities.com/Paris/Rue/4971/*
Finnish: *www.helsinki.fi/~mlang/lewis/*

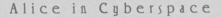

GAMES AND PUZZLES

www.ruthannzaroff.com/wonderland/ Fun for the young.

www.utoronto.ca/ams/recroom/holidaze/easter/xword/alice.htm
An interactive Carrollian crossword puzzle.

ANALYSES

www.gradesaver.com/ClassicNotes/Titles/wonderland/ College-level
summaries, analyses and essays.

www.lewiscarroll.org/bander.html "To Catch a Bandersnatch" is a humorous
ramble through the various interpretations which have been imposed on the
books over the years.

www.salon.com/weekly/carroll960930.html Author Joyce Carol Oates on her
early experience with the books.

www.ucd.ie/classics/2000/imholtz.html Plato in Wonderland.

ILLUSTRATORS

laurenharman.tripod.com/alice This wonderful site, devoted to the many
illustrators, is maintained by a young Carrollian.

oufcnt2.open.ac.uk/~gill_stoker/tenniel.htm The John Tenniel Home Page.

www.exit109.com/~dnn/alice/ Digitized pictures from early illustrators
Attwell, Gutmann, Hudson, Jackson, Kirk and Rackham.

www.bugtown.com/alice/ The Rackham illustrations.

MISCELLANEOUS

www.ezork.com/carrollfont/ Carroll's handwriting from *Alice's Adventures under
Ground* can be downloaded to your computer and used to write letters.

www.thewhiterabbit.com/webring.htm The Alice Web Ring.

www.cs.virginia.edu/~asr4u/madHatter.html Celebrate Mad Hatter Day in
October (U.S.) or June (U.K.)!

www.textarc.org/Alice.html A very unusual way to see the book: on a single page.

Alice Stores & Businesses

ALABAMA Alice's White Rabbit, Birmingham: clothing ♥ Lion & Unicorn Comics and Games, Birmingham ♥ Red Queen Shoppe, Montgomery: gifts

ALASKA Geoffrey the Mad Hatter, Anchorage: clothing

ARIZONA A Mad Hatter's Antiques & Collectibles, Glendale ♥ Mad Hatter Books & Records, Tucson ♥ The March Hare, Wickenburg: restaurant

ARKANSAS Alice's Wonderland Flea Market, Salem

CALIFORNIA The Mad Hatters, Auburn: clothing ♥ Through the Looking-Glass, Berkeley: medical equipment ♥ A Mad Hatter Company, Carlsbad: entertainers ♥ March Hare, Carmel: salon ♥ White Rabbit, Carmel: gifts ♥ White Rabbit Children's Books, Costa Mesa ♥ Mad Hatter, Downey: toys ♥ The Jabberwocky, El Centro: furnishings ♥ Jabberwocky, Eureka: pet supplies ♥ Mad Hatter's Tea Party, Eureka: tea shop ♥ Through the Looking-Glass, Fort Bragg: salon ♥ Humpty Dumpty Kitchen, Grass Valley: restaurant ♥ White Rabbit Children's Books, La Jolla ♥ Mad Hatter Crafts Party & Costumes, Los Angeles ♥ The Jabberwock, Monterey: inn ♥ Cheshire Cat Clinic, Oakland: veterinarian ♥ The Mad Hatter Company, Oceanside: entertainers ♥ Jabberwocky Java, Orange: restaurant ♥ Alice in Wonderland, Oxnard: party supplies ♥ Mad Hatter II Tattoo, Palm Desert ♥ The White Rabbit, San Anselmo: toys ♥ Cheshire Cat Clinic, San Diego: veterinarian ♥ The White Rabbit, San Diego: books ♥ Pat O'Shea's Mad Hatter, San Francisco: bar ♥ Vorpal Gallery, San Francisco: art ♥ Cheshire Cat Books, San Rafael ♥ Cheshire Cat Inn, Santa Barbara ♥ The March Hare Children's Shoppe, Stockton ♥ Mad Hatter, Whittier: salon ♥ Lewis Carroll Academy, Woodland Hills

COLORADO Cheshire Cat, Arvada: restaurant ♥ Brillig Works Café and

Bakery, Boulder ♥ Cheshire Cat Hospital, Broomfield: veterinarian ♥ Jabberwocky, Elizabeth: toys ♥ March Hare, Englewood: gifts ♥ Cheshire Cat Antiques, Evergreen ♥ Through the Looking-Glass, Glenwood Springs: gifts ♥ Mad Hatter Antiques, Leadville

CONNECTICUT Cheshire Cat, Mansfield Center: veterinarian ♥ March Hare Antiques, Plainville ♥ Queen of Hearts, Redding: bakery

DISTRICT OF COLUMBIA The Madhatter, Washington: restaurant

FLORIDA Madhatter's Emporium, Brandon: tea shop ♥ Jabberwocky Restaurant, Brooksville ♥ The Mad Hatter, Cape Coral: gallery ♥ Cheshire Cat, Fort Lauderdale: clothing ♥ The Cheshire Cat, Fort Myers: toys ♥ Through the Looking-Glass, Homestead: salon ♥ A Mad Hatter & Kompany, Homosassa: wedding supplies ♥ Key West Mad Hatter, Key West: hats ♥ Alice's White Rabbit, Panama City Beach: smoking supplies ♥ Mad Hatter Restaurant, Sanibel ♥ Mad Hatter's Tea Room, Tarpon Springs ♥ Through the Looking-Glass Antiques, Tarpon Springs ♥ Alice in Flowerland, Vero Beach: florist ♥ The Mad Hatter, West Palm Beach: bar

GEORGIA The Mad Hatter, Atlanta: club ♥ The White Rabbit, Rome: antiques ♥ The Mad Hatter Tea Shop, Saint Marys ♥ White Rabbit Antiques, Sandersville ♥ Gryphon Tea Room, Savannah ♥ Humpty Dumpty Day Care, Sylvania

IDAHO Walrus & Carpenter Books, Pocatello

ILLINOIS Through the Looking-Glass, Blue Island: antiques ♥ D C Mad Hatter, Chicago: fabrics ♥ Humpty Dumpty, Chicago: restaurant ♥ Mad Hatter, Danville: bar ♥ The Cheshire Cat, Grayslake: gifts ♥ The White Rabbit, Pinckneyville: toys

INDIANA Balloons by Mad Hatter, Columbus ♥ Mad Hatter Custom Hats, Greencastle ♥ Humpty Dumpty's Magazine, Indianapolis ♥ The Cheshire Cat, Madison: consignment ♥ White Rabbit Used Books, Muncie ♥ White Rabbit Store,

Alice Stores & Businesses

New Castle: gifts ♥ Humpty Dumpty Child Care, Palmyra ♥ White Knight Games, Plainfield ♥ Humpty Dumpty Nursery School, Valparaiso

IOWA Madhatter's, Dubuque: bar ♥ Humpty Dumpty Daycare, Humboldt

KANSAS Through the Looking-Glass, Abilene: salon

KENTUCKY Mad Hatter Hat Shop, Lexington ♥ Through the Looking-Glass, Paducah: gifts ♥ White Rabbit Children's World, Versailles: clothing

LOUISIANA The White Rabbit, Shreveport: toys ♥ Cheshire Cat, Sunset: books

MAINE Through the Looking-Glass, Oakland: toys

MARYLAND Alice's Wonderland, Baltimore: salon ♥ Mad Hatter's Cafe, Ocean City

MASSACHUSETTS The Walrus & the Carpenter, Boston: bar ♥ Jabberwocky Children's Shoppe, Chelmsford: clothing ♥ White Knight Records, Great Barrington ♥ White Knight Gallery, New Bedford: gifts ♥ Jabberwocky Bookshop, Newburyport ♥ Mad as a Hatter, Provincetown: gifts, hats ♥ Jabberwocky, Taunton: gifts ♥ Camp Jabberwocky, Vineyard Haven

MICHIGAN Alice's Wonderland, Alma: amusement park ♥ White Rabbit Toys, Ann Arbor ♥ Queen of Hearts, Detroit: amusement park ♥ Mad Hatter, Flint: clothing ♥ Through the Looking-Glass, Kalamazoo: consignment ♥ Queen of Hearts Pastries & Bakery, Saline ♥ White Rabbit Inn, Three Oaks ♥ Through the Looking-Glass, Warren: salon

MINNESOTA The Mad Hatter Tea Room, Anoka ♥ Jabberwocky's Arts & Activities, Crosby ♥ The March Hare, Lanesboro: gifts ♥ Galumph Theatre, Minneapolis: entertainers ♥ Through the Looking-Glass, Owatonna: salon ♥ Frabjous Casual Wear, Saint Cloud ♥ The Mad Hatter, Wilton: bar

343

MISSISSIPPI Queen of Hearts, Jackson: restaurant

MISSOURI Alice's Wicker Wonderland, Cape Girardeau: furniture ♥ The Cheshire Cat, Columbia: toys

MONTANA Madhatter Saloon, Big Timber ♥ Alice's Country Wonderland, Billings: gifts ♥ Through the Looking-Glass, Bozeman: salon ♥ Humpty Dumpty Beads & Sewing, Helena

NEBRASKA Mad Hatter's Coffee & Tea Co., Auburn ♥ Humpty Dumpty Children's & Maternity, Lincoln: consignment ♥ Mad Hatter Hat Shop, Omaha

NEVADA Alice's Wonderland, Boulder City: gifts ♥ Mad Hatter, Winnemucca: clothing

NEW HAMPSHIRE White Rabbit Inn, Allenstown ♥ Dormouse Bakery, Hampton Falls

NEW JERSEY Jabberwocky, Chatham: toys ♥ Humpty Dumpty Drive-In, Columbia: restaurant ♥ Elin's Queens of Hearts, Elizabeth: restaurant ♥ Mad Hatter Antiques, Garfield ♥ Mad Hatter Pub & Eatery, Sea Bright

NEW YORK Mad Hatter Antiques, Binghamton ♥ Cheshire Cat Gift Shop, Cazenovia ♥ Jabberwock, Ithaca: toys ♥ White Rabbit Coffee House, Long Island City ♥ Queen of Hearts, Merrick: bridal ♥ Gryphon Books, New York ♥ Vorpal Gallery Soho, New York: art ♥ Gryphon Record Shop, New York ♥ Mad Hatter Psychic Tea Room, Nyack ♥ Madhatter Bar & Restaurant, Orangeburg ♥ The Cheshire Cat, Potsdam: clothing ♥ Mad Hatter Tavern Inc., Poughkeepsie ♥ Through the Looking-Glass, Ronkonkoma: salon ♥ Gryphon's Pub, White Plains

NORTH CAROLINA White Rabbit Books and Things, Charlotte ♥ Mad Hatter's Bake Shop, Durham ♥ White Rabbit, Greensboro: gifts ♥ White Rabbit Books and

Alice Stores & Businesses

Things, Raleigh ♥ Alice's Wonderland Antiques, Selma ♥ Through the Looking-Glass, Swansboro: florist ♥ Through the Looking-Glass, Wilson: salon

OHIO Mad Hatter, Ashville: antiques ♥ Jabberwocky Tree Farm, Canton ♥ March Hare Salon, Cincinnati ♥ Bill Taylor the Mad Hatter, Cleveland: clothing ♥ Mad Hatter, Cleveland: automobile supplies ♥ The Cheshire Cat, Mechanicsburg: gifts ♥ Mad Hatter's Comedy Theatre, Painesville ♥ Mad Hatter, Toledo: club ♥ Queen of Hearts, Warren: bar

OKLAHOMA Alice's Wonderland Floral Gifts, Broken Arrow ♥ Mad Hatter, Laverne: clothing

OREGON The White Rabbit, Bend: gifts ♥ Queen of Hearts, Newport: lingerie ♥ Cheshire Cat, Portland: cheeses ♥ Queen of Hearts Tavern, Portland ♥ Mad Hatter's Books, Sutherlin

PENNSYLVANIA Queen of Hearts Family Hair Cutters, Ambler ♥ Mock Turtle Marionettes, Bethlehem ♥ Cheshire Cat, Greenville: entertainers ♥ Alice's Wonderland Clothing, Hawley ♥ White Rabbit Cafe, Herndon ♥ Through the Looking-Glass, Jim Thorpe: restaurant ♥ Thru the Looking-Glass, Northern Cambria: salon ♥ The March Hare, Philadelphia: salon ♥ Jabberwocky Books for Kids, Phoenixville ♥ Gryphon Coffee Co., Wayne: café ♥ The White Knights Game Room, Williamsport ♥ Through the Looking-Glass, York: salon

RHODE ISLAND The Walrus & the Carpenter, Middletown: toys ♥ Mad Hatter Bakery, Newport

SOUTH CAROLINA The White Rabbit, Clemson: gifts ♥ Madhatter Magic Novelties and Gifts, Columbia

SOUTH DAKOTA Queen of Hearts Costume & Magic Shop, Rapid City

Alice Stores & Businesses

TENNESSEE Red Queen Custom Tattoos, Chattanooga ♥ Queen of Hearts, Memphis: bar ♥ Queen of Hearts Tattoos, Nashville

TEXAS Alice's Looking-Glass, Amarillo: salon ♥ The Cheshire Cat Resale, Austin: clothing ♥ Mad Hatter's Tea Room, Caldwell: inn ♥ Tweedledee, Canyon, children's clothing ♥ Mad Hatter's, College Station: bar ♥ Jabberwocky Antiques, Fredericksburg ♥ Alice 'N Wonderland, Houston: wigs ♥ Alice's Wonderland Antiques, Kerrville ♥ Alice's Wonderland, Laredo: gifts ♥ Mad Hatter's House of Games, Lubbock ♥ Jabberwocky's, San Angelo: restaurant ♥ Mad Hatter's, San Antonio: restaurant ♥ The Madhatter Hair Studio, San Antonio: salon

UTAH Mad Hatter Gifts, Salt Lake City

VERMONT Mad Hatter, Burlington: restaurant ♥ Jabberwocky Market, Montpelier

VIRGINIA The Looking Glass House, Afton: inn ♥ Brillig Books, Charlottesville ♥ Jabberwocky, Charlottesville: restaurant ♥ Mad Hatter Impressions, Clifton: salon ♥ Jabberwocky Children's Books & Toys, Fredericksburg ♥ Mad Hatter Impressions, Fredericksburg: salon ♥ White Rabbit, Norfolk: consignment ♥ Mad Hatter Impressions, Stafford: salon

WASHINGTON Alice's Wonderland, Kent: florist ♥ Mad Hatter Antiques, Kent ♥ Alice's Looking Glass, Seattle: salon ♥ Cheshire Cat, Vancouver: restaurant

WEST VIRGINIA Jabberwock Café, Beckley ♥ Jabberwock, Elkins: bar

WISCONSIN Jabberwocky, Eagle River: florist ♥ Jabberwocky, Green Bay: toys ♥ Madhatter, Madison: restaurant

347

About the Art

This book includes art from various editions of *Alice's Adventures in Wonderland (AIW)* and *Through the Looking-Glass and What Alice Found There (TTLG)* that have been published around the world. We begin with the most important of all the artists:

Charles L. Dodgson: (background) 68, 184, 188, 189, 196, 197, 200, 201, 202, 216, 225.

John Tenniel: 19, (inset) 39, 71, (inset) 75, (inset) 117, (inset) 120, (border) 177, (border) 184, 210, 250, 252.

John Tenniel and Elenore Abbott, *AIW,* Jacobs: Philadelphia, 1912: 29, 212.

John Tenniel and Hugo Van Hofsten, *AIW,* n.d. (circa 1917): front cover.

After the books fell out of copyright, Tenniel's drawings were copied, hand-colored and sometimes redrawn by a legion of unknown artists: 48, 159, 211, 214, 215, 288, 292, 299.

OTHER ARTISTS FEATURED IN THIS BOOK INCLUDE:

Mabel Lucie Atwell, *AIW,* Raphel Tuck: London, 1910: 33, 55, 58, 100. Background: 75, 134, 275, 294.

A. L. Bowley, *AIW,* Raphael Tuck: London, 1921: 10, 87. Background: 285, 306.

Charles Folkard, *Songs of Alice,* 1920s: 79, 105, 153, 160, 176, 235, 267, 307. Background: 22, 131, 279, 286. Border: 29, 41.

Bessie Pease Guttman, *AIW,* Dodge, New York, 1907: 69.

Gwynedd Hudson, *AIW,* Dodd: New York, 1922: 89, 106, 116, 125, 135, 167, 193, 264.

Franklin Hughes, *TTLG,* Cheshire House: New York, 1931: 28, 223, 273.

A. E. Jackson, *AIW,* Hodder: New York, 1914: 49, 164, 194, 245.

Gertrude Kay, *AIW,* Philadelphia, 1923: 61, 112, 289.

M. L. Kirk, *AIW,* Frederick Stokes: New York, 1904: 45.

Blanche McManus, *AIW and TTLG,* Wessels: New York, 1899: 124, 145, 150, 168, 174, 239, 254, 274, 310, 315.

Helen Monro, *AIW,* n.d.: 82.

John Morton-Sale, *AIW,* London, 1933: 67.

John R. Neill, *Children's Stories That Never Grow Old*, Reilly & Lee: Chicago, 1908: 8, 42, 142, 144, 151, 152, (inset) 299.

Peter Newell, *AIW*, Harper: New York, 1901: 111, 156.

Willy Pogany, *AIW*, New York, 1920s: 182. Background: 13–17.

Edwin John Prittie, *AIW*, Winston Company: Chicago, 1923: 146.

Arthur Rackham, *AIW*, Doubleday: New York, 1907: 137, 139, 165, 187, 277, 304. Background: 35.

Charles Robinson, *AIW*, Cassell: New York, 1907: 64, 70, 77, 115.

Gordon Robinson, *AIW*, Kelley, 1916: 56, 74, 108.

Harry Rountree, *AIW*, Nelson: London, 1908: 122, 293.

D. R. Sexton, *AIW*, Shaw: London: 1930: 132, 256.

Millicent Sowerby, *AIW*, Duffield: New Jersey, 1908: 7, 118, 163, 271, 283.

Margaret Tarrant, *AIW*, Ward Lock: London, 1916: 1, 4, 15, 76, 91, 107, 110, 113, 173, 240, 255, (inset) 288, 296, 303, 308, 309, 311, 319.

W. H. Walker, *AIW*, New York, 1907: 43, 265. Background: 305.

Milo Winter, *AIW*, Rand McNally: Chicago, 1916: (border) 42, 63, (inset) 119, 158, 248, 287. Background: 262, 270, 291. *TTLG*, Rand McNally: Chicago, 1916: 24, (background) 27, 36, 181, 298.

Alice Woodward, *AIW*, Macmillan: New York, 1913: 6, 72, 78. Background: 213.

FEATURED FOREIGN EDITIONS:

Denmark: Lilian Brøgger, *AIW*, 1982: (inset) 92.

Finland: Kuvittanut Tove Jansson, *Liisan seikkailut ihmemaassa*, Albert Bonniers Forlag AB, 1966: 259.

France: M. T. Jallon, *Alice Au Pays des Merveilles*, n.d: 80. Andre Jourcin, *Alice Au Pays des Merveilles*, 1949: 73, 95. A. Pécoud, *Alice Au Pays des Merveilles et A Travers le Miroir*, 1950: 166, 317.

Germany: von F.W. Roth, *Alice in Wunderland*, Nurenberg, n.d: 53, 205, 313, 325.

Italy: Adrienne Ségur, *Alice Nel Paese delle Meraviglie*, 1949: 94. Sergio Rizzato, *Le Adventure di Alice*, Editrice Piccoli: Milan, 1982: (inset) 25.

Japan: Kuniyoshi Kaneko, *Lewis Carroll: Alice's Adventures in Wonderland*, Japan, 1974: 88. Kaneko, *AIW*, Media Factory: Japan, 2000: 279. Goro Kumada, *AIW*, Kodansha: Toyko, 1955: 198, 320. Ken Kuroi, *AIW*, Kumon-Suugaku-Ke: Tokyo, 1982: 46.

Poland: Olga Siemaszko, *Alicja W Krainie Czarow*, Nasza Kseig, 1955: 9, 32, (top) 62, (bottom) 81, 280, 290.

Russia: A. Alfeevskii, *AIW*, StatePrint: Moscow, 1958: (top) 81. Demerova, *Though the Looking-Glass*, 1986: (inset) 65. G. Kalinovskii, *AIW*, Detskaya Literatura: Moscow, 1988: 30. Nikolai Kozlov, *AIW*, Mastastkaya Literatura: Minsk, n.d.: 326. Andrei Martynov, *AIW*, Moscow, 1993: 295. Russian edition of *AIW*, no date: 219.

Sweden: Gosta Knutsson, *Alices Aventyr I Sagolandet och Bakom Spegeln*, Stockholm, 1945: 140, 247.

OTHER IMAGES IN THIS BOOK ARE FROM THE FOLLOWING SOURCES:

Page 1: Background: *AIW* printed textile, circa 1930s. **2,** (border) **328:** Guinness Beer produced many promotional booklets and ads featuring Alice and the other characters from Wonderland. **12:** E. Gertrude Thomson, *The Nursery Alice*, 1890. Cover image. **17:** Photo by Llisa Demetrios, Mill Valley, California, 2003. **18:** Jessie Willcox Smith, *Boys and Girls of Bookland*, David McKay: Philadelphia, 1923. **20, 52, 292:** *AIW*, Juvenile Publications, artist unknown, n. d. (circa 1920s). **23:** Record album cover. Alice songs sung by the Choo Choo Players. "Hi FI for the Small Fry," undated. **26, 40, 96, 276:** A.A. Nash, *AIW*, Juvenile Productions, n.d. **34, 38,** (bottom) **62, 154, 172, 322:** Antique postcards, n.d. **41:** Inset: Charles Pears, 1908. **44, 171:** Unknown illustrator, no date. **50, 284, 301:** *AIW and TTLG*, illustrated with scenes from the Photo Play, The Nonpareil Feature Film Corporation, Grosset and Dunlap: New York, 1918. **60:** Give-away picture card from a package of Lion Coffee, Toledo, Ohio, n.d. **85, 263:** J. G. Sowerby, *Young Maids and Old China*, Ward: London. 1885. **92, 126:** "Alice in Wonderland," Paramount Pictures, 1933. Publicity still featuring Charlotte Henry as Alice, Ford Sterling as The White King, Louise Fazenda as the White Queen, and Baby LeRoy as the Joker. **97, 143, 272, 316:** *TTLG*, unknown illustrator, Boston, n.d. (circa 1910s). **99:** Honor C. Appleton, 1919. **101–103:** Henry Furniss, *Mad Gardener's Song*, 1889. **121:** Painting by Quentin Matsys, National Gallery, London. **128, 148, 242,** (borders) **334–352:** Tony Sarg, *Tony Sarg's Alphabet*, n.d. **130–133:** Randolph Caldecott, *The Queen of Hearts*, Routledge: London, 1881. **175:** "Ellis in Wonderland," Ray Ellis and His Orchestra, album cover, n.d. **180:** Print from London paper, circa 1900. **190:** Henry Furniss, c. 1880s. **191:** Randolph Caldecott, *The Farmer's Boy*, Routledge: London,1880s. **195:** This one of a kind, handwritten and illustrated *AIW* was purchased by Sandor Burstein in 1985. The book was

About the Art

signed: Lawrence Melnick, 1956, Cooper Union. Mr. Burstein attempted to find Mr. Melnick but the school lost track of him after 1975. **202:** Painting by Charles L. Dodgson, 1862. Lovett Collection, Winston-Salem. Reproduced with permission of Charles Lovett and the estate of Lewis Carroll. **204:** Photo of Josephine Hutchinson as Alice in a theatrical production of "Alice in Wonderland." *New York Magazine Playbill*, The New Amsterdam Theatre, 1933. **206:** Graham Robertson, *Nursery Garland Woven by Kitty Cheatham*. G. Shirmer: New York, 1917. **209, 246, 338:** Undated record album cover. **217:** Line drawings by Henry Furniss, c. 1909. **220:** Clipping from *The Boston Herald*, April 30, 1932, found in an old edition of *AIW*. **227:** Cover image from *The Big Little Book of AIW* featuring photos from the 1933 movie. **228:** Covers from *Life Magazine*, April 28, 1947; *Classic Comics*, 1948, and *TV Guide*, 1999. The Madame Alexander "Alice" dolls date from 1930 to 1970 and are part of the Woolsey Ackerman Collection. **229:** "Alice's Adventures in the New Wonderland," is a pamphlet promoting Yellowstone National Park for tourists. **230, 268–9:** Magazine advertisements, dates unknown. **233:** Madame Alexander "Alice doll," c. 1940s. The doll measures 17 inches tall, is made from hard plastic, and features a face modeled after the child actress, Margaret O'Brien. The Woolsey Ackerman Collection. **236:** View of Oxford, 1843. Engraver: Tombleson. **241:** Photograph of Isa Bowman posing as Alice for a theatrical production. Isa Bowman, *The Story of Lewis Carroll Told for Young People by The Real Alice in Wonderland Miss Isa Bowman*, Dutton: New York, 1900. **244:** Gertrude Welling, *AIW*, Sears, 1926. Cover image. **257:** Inga-Karin Eriksson, *The Other Alice* by Christina Bjork, R&S Books, Stockholm, 1993. Reprinted by permission of the artist. **278:** Hugh Gee, *AIW*, London, 1948. **302:** Background line art by George Soper, 1911. **318:** Kay Nixon, "Alice in Wonderland" postcard series, No. 1819, CW Faulkner, 1923. **329:** Movie poster for the 1931 film, *Alice in Wonderland*, which starred Ruth Gilbert as Alice. **330–1:** *Alice in Wonderland*, Paramount Pictures, 1933, with Charlotte Henry as Alice, Alison Skipworth as the Duchess, Cary Grant as the Mock Turtle, and Richard Gallagher as the White Rabbit. **332:** Japanese movie poster, *Alice in Wonderland*, Paramount Pictures, 1933. **333:** Publicity still from *Mrs. Miniver*, 1942. **346:** Vintage 1942 postcard of the Mad Hatter shop, Main Street, Danbury, Conn.

EDITORIAL PERMISSIONS:

All extracts from the letters of Lewis Carroll are reprinted with the kind permission of A.P. Watt Ltd., on behalf of the Trustees of the C. L. Dodgson Estate, Morton Cohen and Richard Gordon Lancelyn Green.

Acknowledgments

Producing *All Things Alice* (and its predecessor *All Things Oz*) is not unlike Alice's adventures in Wonderland; both journeys begin with a giant leap of faith into the unknown abyss. For taking the leap with me, I want to thank everyone at Potter: Annetta Hanna, Lauren Shakely, MarySarah Quinn, Pam Krauss, Maggie Hinders and Laura Motta.

While working on the book, I encountered many strange and curious creatures who offered advice, assistance and directions that were sometimes confusing, if not downright perplexing. Thanks anyway to Steve Condiotti, Richard Glenn, Woolsey Ackerman, Chris Measom, Kenneth Fuller at Marchpane Books in London and Ralph Sims in Seattle, Washington.

Mark Burstein functioned as both my Caterpillar (letting me know when I was wrong) and my Cheshire Cat (directing me where to go). I am grateful for his introductions to many fascinating Carrollians: Alan White (thanks for the tour of Oxford, Alan!), Stephanie Lovett Stoffel, Charles Lovett, Angelica Carpenter, Selwyn Goodacre, Mark Richards of the LCS in England and Judith Evans at A. P. Watt Ltd.

No tea party would be complete without my darling duchesses who shared their time and recipes. I send big love and kisses to Marsha Heckman, Sarah Stewart Zweibach, Sasha Perl-Raver, Betsy Levy and my wonderful sister, Susan Sunshine Dorenter.

Thank you, Lena Tabori and Katrina Webber, for making my calendar. Thank you, Lewis Carroll for, well, everything.

Looking back on the journey, I join Alice in wondering if this was, after all, only a splendid dream. If so, I can't wait to fall asleep again.

Last, I want to add that this book is dedicated to my friend and collaborator, Timothy Shaner, whose brilliant vision brings life and energy to every page he designs. Tim and I have worked on dozens of books together and he always makes my work look far better than it deserves. I would follow Tim down any rabbit hole.

—Linda Sunshine